# PROOF-TEXTS

OF

# ENDLESS PUNISHMENT,

EXAMINED AND EXPLAINED.

---

BY

D. P. LIVERMORE.

---

CHICAGO, ILL.:
D. P. LIVERMORE.
1862.

S. & A. Emerson, Printers, 174 Clark street, Chicago.

# PREFACE.

THE object of this work is to assist the reader to a correct understanding of those controverted passages which are supposed to teach the doctrine of endless punishment. We have given the Bible a thorough examination, and are convinced that this doctrine finds no support in the sacred pages. It is of human origin.

The best heathen writers admit that this doctrine was INVENTED to frighten those who could not be restrained from vice by the punishments of this life! It was regarded by the heathen, as it now is by some professing Christians, as the most efficient motive to deter men from sin.

Cicero, in his seventh oration, p. 207, says that "It was on this account that the ancients INVENTED those *infernal punishments* of the dead, to keep the wicked under some awe in this life, who without them, would have no dread of death itself."

Polybius, who was a celebrated Greek historian, speaking upon this subject, says: "Since the multitude is ever fickle and capricious, full of lawless passions and irrational and violent resentments, there no way left to keep them in order, but by the *terrors of future punishment*, and all the pompous circumstances that attend such kind of FICTION! On which account the ancients acted, in my opinion, with great judgment and penetration, when they CONTRIVED to bring those *notions of the gods and a future state*, into the popular belief."

Strabo, who was a Greek geographer and eminent philosopher, says: "It is impossible to govern women and the gross body of the people, and to keep them pious, holy and virtuous, by the precepts of philosophy. This can only be done by the *fear of the gods*, which is raised and supported by ancient *fictions* and modern prodigies." And again, he says, that "The apparatus of the ancient mythologies was an engine which the legislators employed as *bugbears* to strike a terror into the childish imagination of the multitude."

*Seneca says:* "Those things which make the infernal regions terrible, the darkness, the prison, the river of flaming fire, the judgment seat, etc., *are all a* FABLE, with which the poets amuse themselves, and by them agitate us with VAIN TERRORS!

It is here admitted that the doctrine of endless punishment was an "invention" of the heathen, a "fiction" and a "bugbear" contrived to deter those people from sin, who could not be influenced by the rewards and punishments of this life.

The doctrine of endless punishment, then, being of purely heathen origin, has no claims upon our regard, any more than idolatry, and the belief of the ancient Jews in the transmigration of souls! It forms no part of divine revelation, and we reject it, because it is a pure fiction of the imagination.

We have not been able to introduce every passage which has been urged in support of the doctrine of endless punishment, but we have examined and explained all the prominent texts which are relied upon to prove the doctrine in question, and have shown that they yield no support to this dogma of the church.

In giving our thoughts upon these controverted texts, we have not written so much for the eye of the critic, as to defend the truth. Conscious of its imperfections, we send out this work, with an earnest desire that it may bear some humble part in removing the religious errors of the world and in bringing many souls to the knowledge of the truth.

# CONTENTS.

# EVERLASTING PUNISHMENT.

"And these shall go away into everlasting punishment; but the righteous into life eternal."—MATT. xxv. 46.

PERHAPS no passage of Scripture between the lids of the Bible is brought forward more frequently and confidently to support the doctrine of endless punishment, than the text we now propose to examine and explain. Having given the subject a most careful and critical examination, we are fully persuaded, that multitudes, through a false religious education, are led to believe that the text teaches the doctrine of endless punishment. This doctrine is assumed to be true, and then the passage before us is adduced to prove it! Thousands are religiously educated to believe that *everlasting* means *endless*—their early instruction and all their sectarian prejudices are in favor of such a definition of the word, and hence, when they read of "everlasting punishment," they understand the expression to mean "endless punishment." Such are therefore surprised to learn that *aionios*, here translated *everlasting*, does not necessarily have that signification, that it is *not* the same word in the original which is rendered *endless;* that it is often used in the Scriptures in a *limited* sense, and that its proper signification is *age-lasting.*

Before coming to a direct exposition of the text before us, we ask the attention of the reader to two or three important considerations which have a legitimate bearing upon our subject.

First, The different classes of individuals referred to in the text, are acquitted and condemned on account of their WORKS, and therefore the subject cannot refer to the immortal world; for heaven is not to be attained by *good works!* Eternal life is the pure, free and unpurchased gift of God, and is not of works of righteousness that we have done, lest any man should boast!

The second important consideration to which we invite the reader's attention, is, that the original word *kolasis*, supposed to teach the doctrine of endless punishment, was frequently applied, as lexicographers inform us, to the *pruning of trees.* In this sense, its application here is full of significance. It shows at once the important *object* of punishment, viz.: to improve and benefit man. For what purpose are trees *pruned?* Not to injure them, certainly; but to improve them. Such being clearly the object of punishment, under the government of an all-wise and benevolent God, hence this term *kolasis* was appropriately employed in the text.

Lexicographers define *kolasis* thus: "Punishment, chastisement, correction, the pruning of trees." This "everlasting punishment" (*aionios kolasis*) is designed for some wise and benevolent purpose, not absolutely to injure, but ultimately to benefit and improve those chastened.

Again: The word rendered everlasting (*aionios*) is not the same word as is translated *endless*, and therefore the doctrine of *endless* punishment is not taught in the passage, under consideration. The word *endless*, from *akatalutos*, occurs but once in the Bible, Heb. vii. 16. "After the power of an endless life."

Undoubtedly, if the doctrine of endless punishment were taught in the passage under consideration, a different term would have been chosen than *aionios*, which signifies an *indefinite period of time.* And this remark is equally applicable to the life of the righteous, which is here called "eternal" (*aionios*) and not endless, not *akatalutos.* This shows conclusively, we think, that had the Savior referred to the life-immortal in heaven, which all admit is endless, he would have employed a descriptive term which clearly taught it, and not one of doubtful import!

Another important fact is, that when the Scripture writers set forth the future state of happiness, they employ other terms than *aionios*, rendered in the text everlasting and eternal! Different terms, we find employed for this purpose, which are never connected with punishment. *Aphthartos* is a Greek word, which occurs several times in the New Testament, and means incorruptible, immortal, but is never applied to punishment! We read of "the glory of the *incorruptible* God," Rom. i. 23; and that "the dead shall be raised *incorruptible*," 1 Cor. xv. 52; and of an *incorruptible inheritance*, 1 Peter i. 4; and of the "King eternal and *immortal*," 1 Tim. i. 17; but we never read of *incorruptible* punishment, nor of an *immortal hell!*

*Aphtharsia* is another Greek word which was employed by the sacred writers in a similar sense, to signify *immortal* and *incorruption.* Hence, the "dead are raised in *incorruption*," 1 Cor. xv. 42; and "inherit *incorruption*," verse 50; and "that Christ hath brought life and *immortality* to light," 2 Tim. i. 10. This term, all admit, is never applied to punishment. It describes an endless life, but not an endless death! And yet we are sometimes told that if *aionios*, rendered *eternal* and *everlasting* in the text, does not refer to the future state, there are no terms employed in the Scriptures to describe the future, immortal condition of mankind. There never was a greater mistake, as these remarks show. We have already seen that *akatalutos*, translated *endless* occurs *once* in the Bible, Heb. vii. 16, and is applied to *life*—"After the power of an *endless life.*" But this word is never applied to *death*, or *punishment*, or *misery*.

*Athanasia* is another term employed to signify *immortality*, and occurs three times, as follows: 1 Cor. xv. 53 and 54, and 1 Tim. vi. 16. In each place, it is rendered immortality, but is never applied to punishment or suffering.

We now ask the reader's attention to the definition given by several lexicographers, to *aion* from which the adjective *aionion* is derived, here rendered everlasting:

"DONNEGAN'S DEFINITION.—*Aion*, time; a space of time; life-time and life; the ordinary period of a man's life; the age of man; man's estate; a long period of time; eternity; the spinal marrow; (*eis tan aionia*), to a very long period, to eternity; (*apo aionas*, from, or in the memory of man). *Aionios*, of long duration, eternal, lasting, permanent."

"Pickering's Definition.—*Aion*, an age; a long period of time; indefinite duration; time, whether longer or shorter, past, present, or future; in the New Testament, the wicked men of the age; the life of man. *Aionios*, of long duration, lasting, sometimes lasting through life, as *æternus*, in Latin."

"Schrevelius' Definition.—*English Edition.* *Aion*, an age, a long period of time; indefinite duration; time, whether longer or shorter, past, present or future; also, in the feminine gender, life, the life of man. *Aionios*, of long duration, lasting, sometimes everlasting; sometimes lasting through life, as *æternus*, in Latin."

"Hink's Definition.—*Aion*, a period of time, an after-time, eternity. Comp. Latin, *ævum.* *Aionios*, lasting, eternal, of old, since the beginning."

"Wright's Definition.—*Aion*, time, age, life-time, period, revolution of ages, dispensation of Providence, present world or life, world to come, eternity. *Aionios*, eternal, ancient."

"Giles' Definition.—*Aion*, time, an age, an indefinite period of time, eternity, the spinal marrow. *Aionios*, eternal, ancient."

With such a variety of signification as this word has, all can see that the doctrine of endless punishment can derive no support, simply because *aionios* is applied to it, for the *first* definition given of *aion* by Donnegan, one of the best lexicographers, is "time, a space of time; life-time and life; the ordinary period of a man's life." This certainly falls far shor of proving *endless* punishment! And Pickering's definition of *aionios* is, "of long duration, lasting, sometimes lasting through life." This surely does not prove endless misery! The true meaning of *aionios* is *age-lasting*, or an indefinite period of time. It is applied to things that are endless, but more frequently to things of limited duration. It is the subject to which it is applied that indicates its meaning. If the nature of that subject is endless in duration, that qualifies the meaning of the word and indicates the sense in which we use the term, everlasting. But if the subject to which this term is applied, is of a limited nature, the word has a limited signification. The subject always determines the meaning of the word. We read of the everlasting hills, and the everlasting God, and it is the nature of each subject which determines the meaning of the word. It must, therefore, first be shown that punishment is necessarily endless in duration, before we can determine that the word *everlasting* when applied to it, has any such signification. We have already seen that *kolasis*, here rendered *punishment*, is correction and improvement, and therefore cannot be endless. Everlasting, therefore, when applied to punishment cannot have that signification. As the word *aion* from which *aionios* is derived, did not originally signify *eternity*, or *endless duration*, the Scripture writers would *repeat* the word to express great duration, and sometimes add the adverb *eti*, which means *yet*, *still* or *farther* and *beyond*. "The Lord shall reign (*ton aiona kai ep aiona kai eti*) forever and ever, and farther;" or as Dr. Clarke has it, "forever and MORE!" Again, "They shall shine as the stars (*eis ton aiona kai eti*) forever and ever and FARTHER." Dan. xii. 3. Again, Micah iv. 5, "We will walk in the name of the Lord our God (*eis ton aiona kai epekeina*) forever and BEYOND IT." It would be folly to say that *aion* here means *eternity* or *endless duration*, as there could be nothing farther or beyond it! These considerations will aid us essentially in understanding the subject before us.

We pass now to give what we regard as the correct interpretation of the text and context. The passage before us is the closing part of the parable of the sheep and goats, which is found in connection with a series of illustrations, which composed one unbroken discourse, recorded in the 24th and 25th chapters of Matthew.

All that is recorded in the parable was to be fulfilled, as the 31st verse of the context informs us: "When the Son of man shall come in his glory, and all the holy angels with him, then shall he sit upon the throne of his glory." This language is highly figurative, and cannot therefore bear, as many have erroneously supposed, a literal interpretation. In the sense in which this language was originally employed, the Scriptures clearly show that the coming of Christ in his kingdom and glory, took place in the days of the primitive Christians, and that some who listened to his instructions lived to witness his coming, in the spiritual manifestation of his truth.

For proof upon this point, we refer the reader to the 27th and 28th verses of the 16th chapter of Matthew, which read as follows:

"For the Son of man shall come in the glory of his Father, with his angels; and then he shall reward every man according to his works. Verily I say unto you, There be some standing here, which shall not taste of death, till they see the Son of man coming in his kingdom."

The coming of Christ here spoken of, we think, is the same as is referred to in the 31st verse of the context. In both cases his coming is spoken of as a *glorious* event; he is represented as being attended with angels, and coming to reward men according to their works. He indicated the nearness of the event by saying, "There be some standing here, who shall not taste of death, till they see the Son of man coming in his kingdom."

Similar phraseology is found at the 1st verse of the 9th chapter of Mark:

"And he said unto them, Verily I say unto you, That there be some of them that stand here which shall not taste of death, till they have seen the kingdom of God come with power."

According to the declaration of the great Teacher, some who listened to his instructions should live to see the kingdom of God come with power, or the Son of man coming in his kingdom. Language similar to this may be found in Luke ix. 27:

"But I tell you of a truth, there be some standing here, which shall not taste of death till they see the kingdom of God."

Jesus, in imparting instruction to his disciples in regard to the same event, employed the following language:

"But when they persecute you in this city, flee ye into another; for verily I say unto you, Ye shall not have gone over the cities of Israel till the Son of man be come." Matt. x. 23.

Here is a positive assertion from the lips of the Savior, that the disciples should not go over the cities of Israel, before the coming of the Son of man should take place.

These Scriptures have an important bearing upon the subject before us, as they show when the Son of man came in his kingdom and in his glory. This point established, we know when the events spoken of in the parable of the sheep and the goats took place. He came during the lifetime of some who heard him speak. Not that he came personally, for he never claimed that he would come thus; but he would come in his kingdom and glory, and in the glory of his Father; he would come by the manifestation of his grace and truth. Archbishop Newcome says:

"That any signal interposition in behalf of his church, or in the destruction of his enemies, may be metaphorically called a coming of Christ."

Kenrick says:

"When the prophet Isaiah represents God as about to punish the Egyptians, he speaks of him as riding upon a swift cloud for that purpose. (Isa. xix. 1). In that case there was no visible appearance of Jehovah upon a cloud; but it is the language which the prophet adopted, in order to express the evident hand of God in the calamities of Egypt. The same thing may be said of the language of Christ upon the present occasion."

There was such an intimate connection between the establishment of Christ's kingdom, and the breaking of the Jewish power, that those events are spoken of simultaneously, and one had such an important bearing upon the other, that they are associated together, and embraced in the same purpose as *means and ends.* Doubtless the destruction of that ill-fated city entered into the divine purpose, as a *means* to the advancement of the Word of God, inasmuch as it crippled the persecuting power of the Jews, weakened their opposition to the cause of Christ, so that the Word of God could have free course and be glorified. It entered into the divine purpose as a means to the better establishment of the kingdom of God; but that destruction did not constitute the main object of Christ's coming, and formed no part of his glory. It removed one great obstacle to the establishment of Christianity. Christ's kingdom here refers to the dispensation of grace and truth manifested to the world through him. And we have already seen, that some who heard him speak were to live to see the kingdom of God come with power. The kingdom of God refers here to the system of religion Christ came to establish, the gospel kingdom, which was not fully established till the persecuting

Jews were humbled by the destruction of their magnificent city, their power broken, and they subjugated and dispersed. Then the kingdom of God was fully established in the earth, the Word of God run, had free course, and was glorified, and converts were multiplied to the faith of the Lord Jesus.

It is evident that Christ did not expect his kingdom would fully come, till the Mosaic economy should end, which did not occur till Jerusalem was destroyed, the civil polity of the Jews was taken away, their temple demolished, their altars laid in ruins, and they brought into subjection to another power. THEN should Christ's spiritual kingdom be set up in the earth, and established on the ruins of Judaism. He came with power to demolish the reign of Judaism, and in glory to establish his own spiritual kingdom.

The destruction of Jerusalem was to the disciples a deeply interesting event, for, to them, it was a sign that the kingdom of God should come with power. That we are correct upon this point, appears evident from the language of Luke, chapter xxi. verses 24–32, inclusive, where the destruction of that city is foretold in the following language:

"And they shall fall by the edge of the sword, and shall be led away captive into all nations: and Jerusalem shall be trodden down of the Gentiles, until the times of the Gentiles be fulfilled. And there shall be signs in the sun, and in the moon, and in the stars; and upon the earth distress of nations, with perplexity; the sea and the waves roaring; men's hearts failing them for fear, and for looking after those things which are coming on the earth: for the powers of heaven shall be shaken. And then shall they see the Son of man coming in a cloud, with power and great glory. And when these things begin to come to pass, then look up, and lift up your heads: for your redemption draweth nigh. And he spake to them a parable: Behold the fig tree, and all the trees; when they now shoot forth, ye see and know of your own selves that summer is now nigh at hand. So likewise ye, when ye see these things come to pass, know ye that the kingdom of God is nigh at hand. Verily I say unto you, This generation shall not pass away, till all be fulfilled."

This language throws much light upon the subject. After the disciples were instructed concerning the SIGNS which should precede the destruction of that ill-fated city, Christ says, "So likewise YE, when ye see these things come to pass, know ye that the KINGDOM OF GOD IS NIGH AT HAND." The kingdom of God should immediately succeed the downfall of that city. Then the disciples should lift up their heads, "for your redemption draweth nigh." That is, they were to be delivered from those severe persecutions to which they had been subject for embracing the truth. Their persecutors were humbled, and the kingdom of God was more successfully preached. Dr. Barnes comments thus, on the phrase, "Kingdom of God nigh at hand:"

"That is, from the time God will signally build up his kingdom. It shall be fully established when the Jewish polity shall come to an end; when the temple shall be destroyed, and the Jews scattered abroad. Then the power of the Jews shall come to an end; they shall no longer be able to persecute you; and you shall be completely delivered from all these trials and calamities in Judea."

Having thus learned when Christ was to come in his kingdom, and in the glory of his Father, we ascertain when all the events spoken of in the parable of the sheep and goats took place. We are now prepared to understand the preceding context.

In the preceding chapter, we learn that Jesus had spoken of the destruction of Jerusalem and the terrible fate that awaited the inhabitants of that magnificent city. The disciples desiring more information concerning the fearful calamity to which the Master had alluded, familiarly addressed him in the following language: "Tell us *when* shall these things be? and what shall be the sign of thy coming, and of the end of the world?" (*aion*) or AGE. The word here translated world is *aion*, from which *aionios*, rendered everlasting in the text is derived.

We read of the end of the world, or *aion*, in 1 Cor. x. 11, Heb. ix. 26. This cannot mean eternity, for eternity has no end! The discourse of our Lord recorded in the 24th and 25th chapters of Matthew, contains a full reply to these queries of the disciples. The gospel of the kingdom was to be proclaimed very extensively prior to the destruction of that great city, though not as successfully as afterward. While many would remain faithful to the Master's cause, others, through severe persecution, would turn back again to the weak and beggarly elements of Judaism. From the 5th to the 28th verse, inclusive, of the 24th chapter, Jesus enumerates the SIGNS which should precede the destruction of Jerusalem; and at the 29th verse, he predicts its downfall by saying that the sun should be darkened, the stars fall from heaven, and the powers of the heavens should be shaken. This was in accordance with the ancient mode of speech. Fearful calamities and temporal national judgments were indicated by representing great convulsions in nature. See Isa. xiii. 10; xxxiv.; Ezek. xxxii.; Joel ii.

Jesus then indicates the nearness of the events by the "Parable of the fig tree:" "When it putteth forth leaves we know that summer is nigh; so likewise ye, when ye shall see all these things, know that it is near, even at the doors."

By this similitude, the disciples were instructed in regard to the *end of the world*, (*aion*) or *age*. And to impress this truth still more sensibly upon their minds, he confines the fulfillment of all the things he had mentioned to that generation; verse 34—"Verily I say unto you, this generation shall not pass till all these things be fulfilled." Upon this passage, Dr. Whitby comments as follows:

"These words, *this age* or *generation shall not pass away*, afford a full demonstration that all which Christ had mentioned hitherto, was to be accomplished, not at the time of the conversion of the Jews, or at the final day of judgment, but in that very age, or whilst some of that generation of men lived; for the phrase never bears any other sense in the New Testament, than the men of this age."

The Son of man should come with power and great glory, and should send forth his angels, or ministers, or apostles, to gather together such as had been faithful in different places, where the gospel of the kingdom had been preached. Those who professed his religion are compared to ten virgins; those who were wise gave heed to his instructions, while the foolish turned away from the truth. The object of this parable was to inculcate *watchfulness*, which is followed by another concerning the talents, the moral of which is *faithfulness.* Then the parable of the sheep and goats is introduced, the object of which is to represent the separation that should take place between the wise and faithful and the foolish and unfaithful. Those who remained true and faithful should inherit the gospel kingdom, while those who opposed the gospel and persecuted the disciples, were to suffer in the general calamities which were to come upon the nation. The Christians who were in the enjoyment of gospel privileges, were said to be on the right hand, while the enemies of Christ being in a state of condemnation and misery, were said to be on the left hand. This simply represents the different conditions of the friends and enemies of the truth. The prominent opposers of the Savior's religion, were called the devil and his angels; and after they had filled up the measure of their iniquities, they were to suffer *age-lasting* punishment, while the righteous, or faithful

Christians were in possession of *age-lasting life*, a spiritual life they enjoyed as long as they remained faithful. The subject had no reference to the immortal resurrection world, but exclusive application to this life. The eternal life is the life the believer enjoys in this world by being brought to the knowledge of the truth. "This is life eternal that they might know Thee, the only true God and Jesus Christ whom thou hast sent." John xvii. 3. "He that believeth on the Son HATH everlasting life." John iii. 36, and vi. 47. The true Christian believer lives NOW in the enjoyment of everlasting life.

Thus we see that it is not necessary to go into the future world to enjoy everlasting life, for the true Christian believer is in possession of everlasting life; neither are men obliged to go into the immortal state of existence to suffer everlasting punishment. Both can be experienced in this life; one enjoyed and the other suffered. And as the subject under consideration had no reference to the *future* world, both the life and the punishment referred to, might end in this world. As long as the disciples loved and obeyed their Master, they lived in the enjoyment of eternal life; but when they forgot him, and heeded not his teachings, and he upbraided them for their *unbelief* and *hardness of heart*, (Mark xvi. 14), then they did not enjoy everlasting life. The enemies of Christ suffered everlasting punishment. The severe judgments and calamities to come upon them were spoken of under the figure of fire. The prominent *adversaries* of Christ and their subordinate associates, were called the devil and his angels. Matt. xxv. 41.

The word here rendered *devil* is *diabolos*, which means *adversary*, an enemy or opposer. The prominent persecutors of Christians were called the DEVIL. "Behold the DEVIL shall cast some of you into prison." Rev. ii. 10. Severe national judgments are often spoken of under the figure of *fire* and *furnace of fire*. Isa. ix. 19; Isa. xxxi. 9; Jer. xvii. 27; Ezek. xx. 47–48; Ezek. xxii. 18–22.

The word *aionios* translated "*eternal*" and "*everlasting*" in the text, does not show of itself that, either the life or the punishment is *endless* in duration. It is always the *nature of the subject* to which it was applied that defines its meaning. The hills are called *everlasting*. Gen. xlix. 26. In Habakkuk iii. 6, the mountains are called everlasting, and the ways of God are everlasting. In each case, the nature of the subject defines the meaning of the word. When applied to the mountains it has a limited signification; when applied to God, it is unlimited as God himself. When applied to *punishment*, it has a limited signification, as there is nothing in the nature of punishment, or fire, that is necessarily *endless.*

Although severe judgments were inflicted upon the Jews, so that they were banished from the presence of the Lord, and suffered *age-lasting* punishment, yet Paul assures us that all Israel shall be saved. "For God hath concluded them all in unbelief, that He might have mercy upon all." Rom. xi. 32.

# UNQUENCHABLE FIRE.

"And if thy hand offend thee, cut it off: it is better for thee to enter into life maimed, than having two hands to go into hell, into the fire that never shall be quenched: where their worm dieth not, and the fire is not quenched."—MARK ix. 43, 44.

To UNDERSTAND much of the figurative language of the New Testament, we must appeal often to the Old Testament, and learn in what sense similar phraseology is employed therein.

We should bear in mind, that neither the text nor context affirm that the "worm" and "fire" are in the future, immortal world. This is entirely *assumed*, not proved. True, the passage asserts that the fire shall not be quenched; but a brief allusion to the Old Testament will show that such language was understood by the ancient Hebrews, to refer to things connected with this life, and never to eternity. In proof of this, we appeal, first, to Leviticus vi. 12, 13. The Lord is represented as speaking to Moses, concerning sacrifices and offerings, as follows:

"And the fire upon the altar shall be burning in it; it shall not be put out; and the priest shall burn wood upon it every morning, and lay the burnt offering in order upon it; and he shall burn thereon the fat of the peace-offerings. The fire shall ever be burning upon the altar; it shall never go out."

Here it is distinctly asserted, that the fire kindled upon the altar, in Moses' day, should *never* go out, and yet all admit that it ceased to burn centuries ago! Such language was never understood by the ancient Hebrews, to teach that the fire was endless. And yet, this language is as expressive of endless duration as that which we are considering. One passage affirms, that "the fire shall never be quenched;" the other, that "the fire shall never go out."

Again, in Isaiah xxxiv. 9, 10, we read of the temporal calamities coming upon the land of Idumea, in the following bold figurative style:

"The streams thereof shall be turned into pitch, and the dust thereof into brimstone, and the land thereof shall become burning pitch. It shall not be quenched night nor day; the smoke thereof shall go up forever: from generation to generation it shall lie waste; none shall pass through it forever and ever."

This language is similar to that employed

in the text: "It shall *not* be quenched; the smoke shall go up forever and ever." And all this referred to events long since transpired; to the severe chastisements, judg ments, and temporal calamities then about to come upon the land and people of Idumea. And yet, it is said that the fire shall not be quenched, and the smoke shall go up forever and ever. When it says, that the streams thereof shall be turned into pitch, and the dust into brimstone, and the land become burning pitch—the language is not to be understood literally, but as having reference to national ruin and severe temporal calamities; just as the Revelator spoke of the lake of fire and brimstone, to denote the severe national judgments about to come upon Jerusalem, greater, as the Savior declared, than ever had been or ever should be again, which overwhelmed that magnificent city in ruin, which destruction is called their *second* death.

Of Jerusalem, it is recorded in Jeremiah xvii. 27, thus: "I will kindle a fire in the gates thereof, and it shall devour the palaces of Jerusalem, and it shall not be quenched." This figurative language was employed to portray divine judgments coming upon Jerusalem in this life.

Another instance of this bold, figurative

style of speech among the ancients, may be found in Ezekiel xx. 47, 48:

"And say to the forest of the south: Hear the word of the Lord. Thus saith the Lord God: Behold, I will kindle a fire in thee, and it shall devour every green tree in thee, and every dry tree; the flaming flame shall not be quenched; and all faces from the south to the north shall be burnt therein. And all flesh shall see that I, the Lord, have kindled it; it shall not be quenched."

Although it is here distinctly asserted, that the fire shall not be quenched, yet no intelligent man understands the language literally. Learned divines and commentators apply this passage to temporal judgments, which were to come upon Jerusalem.

We think that Dr. Adam Clarke, the Methodist commentator, has given the true interpretation to this passage. He says:

"The forest of the south field is the city of Jerusalem; which was as full of inhabitants as the forest is of trees. I will kindle a fire, i. e., I will send war; and it shall devour every green tree, i. e., the most eminent and substantial of the inhabitants; and every dry tree, i. e. the lowest and meanest also; it shall not be quenched, i. e. till the land be utterly ruined."

We would call the reader's attention to the interpretation of this learned orthodox divine, of the expression—"The fire shall not be quenched, i. e. till the land be utterly ruined." It had no reference to the immortal world; only to temporal ruin.

Having thus seen in what sense such figurative language as is found in the text was employed, in the Old Testament, we pass to consider more particularly its meaning and specific application. The original word, here translated hell, is *gehenna*. It occurs twelve times in the New Testament, and is invariably applied to the Jews, and never once to the Gentiles! This is a remarkable fact, and unaccountable neglect and omission on the supposition that the Gentiles were in danger of *gehenna* fire! Paul was a preacher to the Gentiles, as he himself informs us, in faith and verity; and yet, in all his fourteen epistles, we find no mention made of hell. Once he speaks of the destruction of *hades*. He was a faithful preacher, and declared the whole counsel of God, and he certainly would have threatened the Gentiles with *gehenna* fire had this constituted any part of the divine counsel. But this word hell is not found in any of Paul's epistles, nor even in John's gospel, which was written for the benefit of the Gentiles. Had the Gentiles been in danger of *gehenna* fire, it is fair to presume that they would have been warned against it. Hebrew scholars tell us that *gehenna* is derived from two Hebrew words, *Gee*, which means land, and *Hinnom*, the name of the individual who owned the land —meaning, land of Hinnom. This land, or vale of Hinnom, bordered upon the south-east part of Jerusalem, where it is still represented on all correct maps of Palestine.

We learn from the Old Testament, that, in this valley of Hinnom, sacrifices were offered, by the sinful and idolatrous Jews, to an idol-god, called Moloch. This idol, which had the head of an ox and the body of a man, being hollow, was heated with fire within, and upon its arms its benighted worshipers laid their children, and there they were burned to death. This horrid place was sometimes called Topheth—the name being derived, as some think, from a word signifying *drum*, because drums were beaten to drown the shrieks of the burning children.

To destroy idolatry among the Jews, King Josiah caused this place to be defiled, and looked upon, by the Jews, with abhorrence and loathing, by making it the receptacle of all the filth and offal of the city of Jerusalem. Some writers tell us that the carcasses of beasts and the bodies of criminals were cast into *gehenna*. That this putrifying mass might not taint the atmosphere, fires were kept constantly burning, to consume this offal and garbage thrown into this valley. And as those parts which remained unconsumed would necessarily breed worms, hence came the expression—"where their worm dieth not, and the fire is not quenched."

In proof of what is here asserted in regard to the valley of Hinnom, we refer the reader to 2 Kings xxiii. 10:

"And he [Josiah] defiled Tophet, which is in the valley of the children of Hinnom, that no man might make his son or daughter to pass through the fire to Moloch."

Here, reference is made to the Jews offering human sacrifices to their idol god. After this place was thus defiled, and came to be regarded with so much detestation and loathing, it was employed figuratively to represent temporal calamities. It was perfectly natural for a Jew to say of any guilty wretch—"He ought to be cast into *gehenna*"—thus making this place an emblem of punishment coming upon the sinful in this life. It was referred to by the prophets to denote severe national judgments. Jeremiah speaks of the desolation of Jerusalem as follows:

"I will break THIS CITY, as one that breaketh a potter's vessel that cannot be made whole again, and I will bury them in Tophet till there is no place to bury. Thus will I do unto this place, saith the Lord, and to the inhabitants thereof, and even make this city as Tophet, and the houses of Jerusalem, and the houses of the King of Judah shall be defiled as the place of Tophet." Jer. xix.

These Scriptures indicate clearly that *gehenna* was employed, in the Old Testament, to represent temporal calamities and national judgments to come upon Jerusalem. We are not informed by the sacred penman, that it is employed in any new or different sense. It is referred to as though the people addressed perfectly understood its meaning, and had any new signification been given to the term, the presumption is that the people would have been so informed.

In confirmation of what we have said, we call the attention of the reader to a passage found in the last chapter of Isaiah, the last verse, which reads as follows:

"And they shall go forth, and look upon the carcasses of the men that have transgressed against me: for their worm shall not die; neither shall their fire be quenched; and they shall be an abhorring unto all flesh."

There is such a similarity between the phraseology of this passage and the one under consideration, that some suppose that our Lord had this Scripture in his mind when he uttered the text. Both speak of the worm dying not, and the fire not being quenched, and both refer to severe temporal calamities.

Eminent orthodox divines admit that these expressions have reference to this world. Dr. Parkhurst, of the orthodox church, says thus:

> "Our Lord seems to allude to the worm which continually preyed on the dead carcasses that were cast out into the valley of Hinnom, *gehenna*, and to the perpetual fire kept up to consume them."

And the late Prof. Stuart, of Andover, Mass., an eminent orthodox theologian, says:

> "In the valley of Hinnom, *gehenna*, perpetual fire was kept up, in order to consume the offal which was deposited there; and, as the same offal would breed worms, hence came the expression—where the worm dieth not and the fire is not quenched."

We have already seen that Tophet was a place in the valley of Hinnom, where sacrifices were offered to an idol-god, called Moloch; and of Jerusalem it was said: "I will make *this city* even as Tophet," which denoted, simply, the desolation and fearful judgments coming upon that wicked city. In this sense it is referred to in the text.

We are now prepared to understand the language under consideration, and its relevancy to those to whom it was addressed.

"If thy hand offend thee, cut it off," etc. This being highly figurative language, the literal hand is referred to only by way of illustration.

The meaning evidently is this: let nothing prevent you from embracing my truth and system of religion and becoming my disciples, though dear to you as a member of your body—dear as a hand or an eye. As though the Savior had said: "Here is my kingdom of truth and righteousness, with its blessed principles and soul-inspiring hopes; now part with everything sooner than part with me and my truth." Those who embraced the Savior's religion, and became subjects of his spiritual kingdom, entered into life. Such passed from death unto life; from moral blindness and spiritual darkness into the marvelous light of divine truth. It was better thus to enter into life, to embrace Christ's gospel, even if called to part with friends and houses and lands, than to reject Christ and his religion, and suffer in those terrible judgments which would come on that ungodly people, figuratively represented by *gehenna* fire.

In the days of Christ, many did not embrace his religion, on account of the deep-rooted hostility to his cause, and the opposition such received from their friends, who madly and bitterly persecuted them for following the despised Nazarene. It required great moral courage, in the primitive days of Christianity, to become one of Christ's disciples. Those who embraced his religion were called upon to make great personal sacrifices. Many did not confess him through fear of being cast out of the synagogue; for they loved the praise of men more than the praise of God. Kindred and friends opposed all who became his followers: so that the father was set against the son, and the daughter against the mother, and the daughter-in-law against the mother-in-law, and a man's foes were those of his own house. All this was known to the Savior; and yet he says that it is better to enter into life thus maimed, thus persecuted and forsaken, than to reject the truth, and suffer in those direful woes about to come upon that sinful nation. Jesus would have his disciples forsake all for him, father and mother, if need be, and houses and lands.

Though his followers were called to suffer the loss of all things, though the hand of persecution might be raised by kindred and friends, yet, better enter into life *thus maimed*, than to cling to those friends and share with them the judgments of God, figuratively represented by *gehenna* fire. Jesus required his disciples to forsake all for him. He said: "Whoso loveth father or mother more than me, is not worthy of me." Those who loved ease and fame and popularity more than him and his unpopular cause, were not worthy of him. As though Jesus had said: "In embracing my cause, now unpopular, now scorned and rejected by the world, the chief priests and rulers, you may be called to part with something, dear to you as a member of your body; some dear friend may turn coldly from you and forsake you; it may be like severing a limb from the body; like cutting off a hand, or plucking out an eye; yet, better enter into life thus maimed; better cherish the hope of everlasting life at this great sacrifice, than to reject the truth, and remain in a state of unbelief and moral blindness."

If thy hand offend thee, or cause thee to offend, cut it off. That is, if one, dear to you as a hand, should cause you to offend against the truth, and abandon Christ, turn away from such, though dear to you as a member of your body. Better enter into life thus maimed; better embrace the truth at this great sacrifice, than suffer in those judgments which will come upon those who reject the truth.

Fidelity to Christ and his cause, under all circumstances, is the practical sentiment here inculcated. We should adhere firmly to the truth under all the trials and persecutions of the world. Though his truth may be never so unpopular, yet we should bind it to our hearts as the pearl of great price, and be ready to exclaim with the poet,—

"Should all the forms that men devise
Assault my faith with treacherous art,
I'd call them vanity and lies,
And bind the Gospel to my heart."

Though friends, whom we love, may assault our faith, and turn coldly from us, yet we are not ashamed of the gospel of Christ; that gospel which is good news of great joy unto all people. We are willing to labor and suffer reproach for trusting in the living God, who is the Savior of all men. Many of us have embraced the doctrines of the great Teacher through much tribulation and persecution. Some of our friends and kindred have forsaken us; have called us hard names —infidels and heretics. Though we have suffered the loss of many things dear to us, yet we have felt it better thus to enter into life, and have the peace of God, which passeth knowledge, and the sweet approbation of our own consciences. God help us to be faithful to our own enlightened convictions, and own Christ as the Savior of the world, unto whom every knee shall bow, and every tongue confess that he is Lord, to the glory of God, the Father.

# THE SECOND DEATH.

"And I saw the dead, small and great, stand before God; and the books were opened, and another book was opened, which is the book of life; and the dead were judged out of those things which were written in the books, according to their works.

"And the sea gave up the dead which were in it; and death and hell delivered up the dead that were in them, and they were judged every man according to their works. And death and hell were cast into the lake of fire. This is the second death."—REV. xx. 12-14.

AS MANY erroneous ideas have been entertained in regard to this language of the Revelator, and as many mistaken opinions still prevail concerning the second death, we propose to give the subject a thorough examination.

Human creeds teach that endless misery is the second death which man is to suffer in the immortal world. It is believed that the term "hell," "lake of fire," and "second death," do not refer to different places or states of being, but all have reference to the same place and denote the same awful state of suffering after death.

Now, on the supposition that "HELL" means a place of suffering in the immortal world, as many contend, it cannot be *endless* in duration, for death and hell delivered up the dead that were in them; hence, if delivered from hell, as the Revelator informs us, the suffering certainly was not endless! Besides, we are nowhere informed that those delivered from hell returned back again. But it is not essential to dwell at length upon the errors into which many have fallen upon this subject, and hence we pass to other considerations.

Some have thought that apostatizing from the faith was the second death. Man is represented in the Bible as being dead in trespasses and sins, and when such have been quickened, born of God, and renewed in the spirit and temper of their minds, and been transformed into newness of life by the spirit of grace and truth, and have afterwards fallen away — backslidden from the faith — and turned back again to the weak and beggarly elements of the world, they are spoken of by an apostle as being twice dead, or suffering a second death. All this is doubtless true, and such might suffer not only a second but a third and fourth death, for as often as they should fall back from a moral quickening, or moral life, they would be dead in sin again. This exposition of the subject does not appear to us to be what the Revelator intended by the second death, referred to in our text. A more obvious and natural interpretation to our mind is that a national death is spoken of, a temporal destruction, which was to come upon the Jewish nation soon after the book of Revelations was written; a destruction more severe than had ever visited a nation, and greater indeed than ever should be again. It is proper here to remark that we think the book of Revelations was written previously to the second destruction of Jerusalem by the Romans. While learned and distinguished biblical divines do not agree upon this point, we think there is sufficient evidence in the book itself to warrant the belief that it was written prior to the second overthrow of the Jewish nation by Titus, and the dispersion of the chosen people of God among the nations of the earth.

In the short preface to the book of Revelations, we are twice informed, that what was contained in the book itself was soon to be accomplished — the time was near at hand for the fulfillment of the vision. In the first verse we are informed that Jesus Christ revealed unto his servants things which must shortly come to pass. And in the third verse, those who heard and read the prophecy, were commanded to keep and treasure up those things which were written — they were near — not far off — but at hand. And after the vision had been made known, to remind the people again that the things written were soon to be fulfilled, we read as follows in the last chapter of this book:

"Behold I come quickly; and my reward is with me, to give to every man according as his work shall be. He which testifieth these things, saith — *surely I come quickly*."

This language clearly indicates to our mind that the prophecies contained in this book were soon to come to pass, and not that untold ages were to elapse before they should be fulfilled. In olden time the prophets were commanded to seal up the saying of their prophecy, when the time was not at hand, or when the things prophesied were not soon to be fulfilled. But when the events predicted were soon to be accomplished, the vision was commanded not to be sealed, for the time was at hand. Hence the Revelator was NOT to seal up the words of his prophecy, for the time of fulfillment was near at hand. "Seal not the sayings of the prophecy of this book, for the time is at hand." Rev. xxii. 10.

In Revelations, Christ is represented as coming quickly—and "coming in clouds and all the kindreds of the earth shall wail because of him." Throughout the Evangelists similar language is employed to represent the second overthrow of the Jewish nation and the coming of the Lord Jesus Christ.

"And then shall appear the sign of the Son of man in heaven; and then shall all the tribes of the earth mourn, and they shall see the Son of man coming in the clouds of heaven with power and great glory." Matt. xxiv. 30.

The Revelator says, "Behold, he cometh with clouds;" Matthew says, "The Son of man cometh in the clouds of heaven." The Revelator says, "And all the kindreds of the earth shall wail because of him;" Matthew says, "And then shall all the tribes of the earth mourn." Both have reference to the second destruction of the Jewish nation.

The context sets forth in highly figurative language the awful woes and calamities which were to come upon the house of Isreal as a retribution for sin. What has been predicted was all summed up in this phrase—"This is the second death." And hence this language clearly implies that there must have been a death previous to this, somewhat similar in its nature. As this national death of the Jews is called the second death, there would be no propriety in this language unless they had suffered a death before this; for if the Revelator were describing their first national death, he certainly would not have described the terrible judgments coming upon the Jewish nation as their second death. It is evident, therefore, that the people referred to must have suffered a death previous to this. We find upon examination that it was so. They had once before lost their national life, and consequently died a national death. That was their first death. And as the Revelator describes more overwhelming calamities to come upon them and greater destruction, he very properly speaks of it as their second death.

The second death was the second destruction of the Jews by Titus, a Roman general, who successfully led the Roman army against the Jewish people, and destroyed them as a nation, so that they have been suffering everlasting punishment for the last eighteen hundred years. Then they lost their national power, and national existence for the second time; and losing their national life the second time, it was called their *second* death. Their *first* destruction was when they were led into Babylonish captivity for seventy years—then they lost their national existence and were said to be dead. Then they were led away from their religious altars and became subject to heathen despots. That calamity constituted their *first* national death. They had no national existence as before. Their restoration from this captivity to their land again, to their altars and temple worship, is spoken of as a resurrection to life. It was like coming up out of their graves; hence, said the Lord, referring to their deliverance, "I will open your graves, and cause you to come up out of your graves, and bring you into the land of Israel." They are represented not only as being dead, but as being in their graves. For instruction upon this point, we refer the reader to the 37th chapter of Ezekiel, verse 12–14:

"Therefore prophesy and say unto them, Thus saith the Lord God; Behold, O my people, I will open your graves, and cause you to come up out of your graves, and bring you into the land of Israel. And ye shall know that I am the Lord, when I have opened your graves, O my people, and brought you up out of your graves; And shall put my spirit in you, and ye shall live, and I shall place you in your own land: then shall ye know that I the Lord have spoken it, and performed it, saith the Lord."

Here we learn that the Jews, or house of

Israel, are represented as being slain and in their graves, but they were to come up out of their graves and live again in their own land, as the 14th verse informs us.

This is highly figurative language, and must not be understood literally. It represents the low state of the Jewish people during their seventy years' captivity. While yet individually alive, their were nationally dead and in their graves. But after they were delivered from captivity and restored to their national privileges and religious altars, they again became a haughty, proud and rebellious people, and ultimately filled up the measure of their iniquity by crucifying the Lord's Anointed and put him to an open shame. Again were severe national judgments to come upon them, and they were to lose their national privileges and national life; and this was their second death.

The highly figurative language employed to describe the second death was in accordance with the ancient mode of speech. Temporal destruction and the overthrow of nations were described, by representing nature as undergoing great changes — the sun being darkened, and the moon turned into blood, and the stars falling from heaven.

"Fire" was another common figure chosen

to set forth direful woes and severe national judgments and calamities. Perhaps no figure was more common among the ancients than this. The Jews are spoken of in the Old Testament as being cast into a furnace of fire, and we are twice informed that the Lord's fire is in Zion, and his furnace in Jerusalem!

This lake of fire was a figurative expression designed to represent the terrible national calamities coming upon the house of Israel. We find similar phraseology throughout the Scriptures. In the 22d chapter of Ezekiel, 17th to 22d verses inclusive, we read as follows:

"And the word of the Lord came unto me, saying, Son of man, the house of Israel is to me become dross: all they are brass, and tin, and iron, and lead, in the midst of the furnace; they are even the dross of silver. Therefore, thus saith the Lord God, Because ye are all become dross, behold, therefore, I will gather you into the midst of Jerusalem. As they gather silver, and brass, and iron, and lead, and tin, into the midst of the furnace, to blow the fire upon it, to melt it; so will I gather you in mine anger and in my fury, and I will leave you there, and melt you. Yea, I will gather you, and blow upon you in the fire of my wrath, and ye shall be melted in the midst thereof. As silver is melted in the midst of the furnace, so shall ye be melted in the midst thereof; and ye shall know that I, the Lord, have poured out my fury upon you."

This again is highly figurative language, descriptive of the severe temporal judgments to come upon the Jewish people. The people were to be gathered in the midst of Jerusalem, as the 19th verse informs us, and the next words are, "And I will leave you there [that is, in Jerusalem] and melt you." The meaning of this is, that the people should be visited with fearful woes and severe national judgments. In the 9th chapter of Isaiah, we read that the wickedness burneth as the fire, and the people shall be as the fuel of the fire, the meaning of which is, that they should be destroyed. In the 34th chapter of Isaiah, we have an account of a great slaughter in the land of Idumea. The destruction should be great, and the slaughter terrible, so that the smell should be offensive and the slain should be cast out. At the 9th verse, what was to occur is figuratively described as follows: "And the streams thereof shall be turned into pitch, and the dust thereof into brimstone, and the land thereof shall become burning pitch." This was highly figurative language, and denoted simply national ruin and destruction.

It was no new thing for the Revelator to represent the overthrow and destruction of a nation, by such figurative expressions as "fire," and even "lake of fire." Regarding then the second death as the second destruction of the Jewish nation by the Romans, we come to a more specific consideration of the subject.

"I saw the dead, small and great, stand before God, and the books were opened," etc. This refers to those who rejected Christ, and spurned his teachings and religion. Rejecting his gospel, their names were not written in the book of life, that is, they did not embrace the gospel of life and immortality. The gospel of Christ was the book of life. Those whose names were found written therein, were such as embraced the gospel, by faith and made practical its divine teachings. They suffered not the second death. They did not suffer in those calamities which come upon that ungodly race—not a Christian perished in those national judgments. Those who endured faithful to the end were saved as the Savior promised.

The books were opened, out of which the dead were judged. These doubtless referred to the books of the Jewish laws to which even the Jews had been unfaithful, they having made void the law of God by their traditions, and taught for doctrines the commandments of men. They were judged out of those things written in the books, according to their works.

"And the sea gave up the dead which were in it, and death and hell delivered up the dead which were in them." The meaning of this language is, that nothing could screen the people from impending judgments and a righteous retribution. After they had filled up the measure of their iniquity, in vain could they seek concealment anywhere. In vain would they cry to the rocks and mountains to fall on them and hide them. They must then be brought to judgment and punished. Similar language is found in the book of Amos ix. 2, 3.

"Though they dig into hell (*sheol*), thence shall my hand take them, and though they climb up to heaven, thence will I bring them down; and though they hide themselves in the top of Carmel, I will search and take them out thence; and though they be hid from my sight in the bottom of the sea, thence will I command the serpent, and he shall bite them."

This language was designed to teach simply that the people could not conceal themselves from the retributive justice of God.

In vain would they seek refuge in death and hell (*sheol*). Their covenant with death should not stand, and their agreement with hell should be disannulled. Dr. Adam Clarke remarks as follows upon this passage:

"*Though they dig into hell*—though they should get into the deepest caverns; though they climb up to heaven—get to the most inaccessible heights—I will drag them up from the one, and pull them down from the other. Though they hide themselves—all these are metaphorical expressions, to show the impossibility of escape."

In the same metaphorical sense, we think the language we are considering should be understood; and when it says that the sea gave up the dead which were in it, and death and hell, or *hades*, gave up the dead which were in them—it means simply that nothing would screen the guilty from righteous retribution; they should be judged according to their works, and punished for their sins. There should be no escape after they had filled up the measure of their iniquity, and merited retribution. Severe national judgments should come upon them, and they again should be dispersed—lose their national life—and be cast out as a by-word and reproach among the nations of the earth, and suffer everlasting punishment.

The same general sentiment is taught, we think, in the 21st chapter, at the 8th verse, where we are informed that the fearful and unbelieving, and murderers, sorcerers, and idolaters, etc., should have their part in the lake which burneth with fire and brimstone —which is the *second death.* When the Jewish nation suffered destruction for the second time—which, indeed, was their second national death—the Christians were saved from these impending judgments—their names were written in the book of life—that is, they gave heed to the instruction of Christ, obeyed his commands, had passed from death unto life, and consequently were not hurt of the second death; they escaped those judgments which came upon the ungodly Jews, while those who rejected Christ and his teachings had their part in the lake of fire and brimstone—which is the second death. No one pretends to understand this language literally. It is highly figurative, and refers to the direful woes and severe national calamities which were to come upon the Jewish race, greater than ever had been or should be again.

Again—"Blessed and holy is he that hath part in the first resurrection." Those who had been quickened from dead works to serve the living God, through the Savior's teachings, were said to be morally and spiritually raised. "*Awake* thou that sleepest and *arise from the dead*," etc. The Christians did thus rise from their dead state—they were once dead in trespasses and in sins—when quickened they were raised from the dead, from their state of moral, spiritual death, and thus had part in the first resurrection. And on such the second death had no power. Enduring unto the end faithful, they were saved from sin, and saved from the woes which came upon the unfaithful and unbelieving. Eusebius, the historian, says that not a Christian suffered. They were priests of God, true and faithful followers of Christ, and were exalted to a high rank in the Christian church, and live and reign with Christ.

# SALVATION AND DAMNATION.

"Marvel not at this: for the hour is coming, in the which all that are in the grave shall hear his voice, and shall come forth; they that have done good unto the resurrection of life; and they that have done evil unto the resurrection of damnation."—JOHN v. 28, 29.

It is supposed by many that this passage of Scripture is descriptive of scenes and events which are to take place at the resurrection of man from the dead, when, it is thought, the whole universe of intelligent beings will be raised bodily and be brought to judgment. Here, it is said, we are expressly informed that a portion of the human race will be raised from the dead to immortal life and blessedness; and another portion of the intelligent creation will be raised bodily, and consigned to the regions of dark despair, to wail and writhe in ceaseless anguish! It is affirmed, that the resurrection of life spoken of, has direct reference to the felicity which awaits the righteous in heaven; and that the resurrection of damnation refers to the awful misery which will be inflicted on such as die impenitent and sinful. Hence, it is said, that this Scripture teaches the doctrine of rewards and punishments in the immortal world—for the good and evil deeds of this life. Such, in brief, is the popular interpretation of this language of the Savior. We regard it as unwarrantable and objectionable for the following reasons:

1. It is based entirely upon assumption, and takes for granted the very thing to be proved! It assumes that a time is coming in the divine economy, when there will be a general resurrection of man, bodily, from the grave. But does this scripture furnish the least proof of such a sentiment? Far from it. This is taken for granted. Many suppose and conscientiously believe, that it teaches such a doctrine; but the language employed will not justify such a conclusion. It does not say that the material body is to be raised from the dead; nor that all men are to be judged in the future world; nor that some will be rewarded with eternal life and felicity for their good works, and some punished with eternal misery for their wicked deeds. If these doctrines are true, we think that every unprejudiced mind must acknowledge, that other testimony and evidence must be relied upon to prove them true.

People first believe these doctrines, and then introduce this scripture as furnishing proof of the sentiments embraced. True, it speaks of a resurrection of life and a resurrection of damnation; but it says nothing concerning the resurrection of the body. Such a resurrection is no where spoken of in the Scriptures as applying to mankind. The resurrection of the material body — the same identical particles of matter — appears to be an unphilosophical and unscriptural sentiment. The question is asked, "How are the dead raised up? and with what body do they come?" Paul, in answer to that query, says, "Thou sowest not that body that shall be... It is sown a *natural* body; it is raised a *spiritual* body. That which is first is natural; afterward, that which is spiritual." Such is the Scriptural doctrine concerning the immortal resurrection of man from the dead.

Again, this passage does not inform us that the resurrection is simultaneous and general, as popular theology asserts. It speaks of those only who are in their graves. Now, on the supposition that the grave here means the ground, it only proves that such as have been buried in the earth shall be raised. If it is to be understood literally, it is far from embracing all mankind — having no relation to those who shall be upon the earth at the last day — who, instead of seeing corruption, it is said, will be caught up to meet the Lord in the air. Thus we see that what should be proved in relation to this scripture, is assumed and taken for granted without proof.

2. The popular exposition of this text is logically untrue, and hence it is objectionable. In making it teach endless rewards and punishments, it proves too much, and hence logically proves nothing! It would prove universal salvation and universal damnation! It is affirmed that the resurrection of life spoken of, means ceaseless happiness in heaven; and the resurrection of damnation means ceaseless misery. Bearing this interpretation in mind, let us attend to the language employed: "They that have done good shall come forth to the resurrection of life;" that is, to eternal bliss in heaven. Now, who have done good? All certainly have done some good in their life-time; then all will be rewarded with eternal life, if the passage has a universal application; for all have done good. No particular kind of goodness is here specified; but simply, that they have done good shall come forth to the resurrection of life. Every human being,

though never so depraved, has done some good; hence, all shall be blessed with immortal life, if the popular exposition of this passage be correct! So on the other hand, universal damnation is as easily and as logically proved true: "For they that have done evil, shall come forth to the resurrection of damnation." If damnation here means endless wretchedness and pain, then all men must be eternally lost, for all men have done evil. If any deny that all have done good, it will be readily and universally admitted, that all have done evil. And the broad declaration is, that they have done evil shall come forth to the resurrection of damnation! Thus we see that the argument logically proves too much, and consequently proves nothing.

The objector cannot extricate himself from this dilemma, by affirming that some repent before they die; for this text does not say, that all shall come forth to the resurrection of damnation, who do not repent before they die; but they that have done evil shall thus come forth; and as all have done evil, so all must be damned, according to the popular interpretation.

3. The common exposition of this scripture makes immortal blessedness depend upon good works; and this sentiment receives no

support from the word of God. According to the passage under consideration, some were to come forth to the resurrection of life, because they had done something that was good; not because they had embraced the true faith, nor on account of the abundant mercy of God; but on account of their good deeds: "They that have done good," etc. This is not only opposed to the Scriptures, but opposed to the sentiments advocated by the dominant sects themselves. They have long made doctrine the test of a man's Christianity; if he has not had an evangelical faith, he has been denounced an infidel. This is the method employed by all the popular churches to ascertain whether a man is a Christian or not. If he does not believe a creed, and certain established doctrines, he is hurled out of the church as unworthy of Christian membership, and consequently is regarded as unworthy of heaven, and only fit for hell! Such, it is said, will come forth to the resurrection of damnation. Thus faith is made the standard, and not good works. It matters not how kind and benevolent and good a man is, if he have not the true faith, he must be lost. All his morality will only sink him lower into perdition.

Thus we see that if this scripture relate to

immortal blessedness, it is to be merited by good works. But this is opposed to the Bible doctrine of a heavenly immortality. Heaven is spoken of as the gift of God; and is not to be attained by good works, but by the abundant mercy of the Infinite Father. We are nowhere informed that man is to be blessed with a resurrection to immortal life, because he has done good; neither that he is to be sent to an endless hell of suffering because he has done evil.

4. The last objection we now present against the popular view of the passage under examination, is, that it does not harmonize with other portions of the Scriptures which describes the immortal resurrection of man from the dead. It does not agree with the state and condition of man in the resurrection world, as set forth by the Savior and the apostle Paul, who was divinely instructed in relation to the doctrines he taught.

Christ, speaking of the condition of men in the resurrection world, says that they shall be equal unto the angels in heaven; (Luke xx. 35, 36); and Paul declares that in Christ shall all be made alive; (1 Cor. xv. 22); and that there is no condemnation to such as are in Christ. (Rom. viii. 1). Now, if all who died in Adam shall be made alive in Christ, and made equal unto the angels of God in heaven, as the Bible teaches, how can such as have done evil be made endlessly wretched? If the common view of the passage we are considering be correct, then the Scriptures contradict themselves; but it evidently has no reference to the immortal resurrection of man.

Paul not only informs us that all shall be made alive in Christ, but he had hope towards God for the resurrection of all. But how could he have hoped for the resurrection of all men, if he believed that a part of the intelligent creation would writhe in ceaseless agony? Could he have hoped for their eternal wretchedness? Never! Had he believed that the resurrection of damnation spoken of, referred to endless woe, he never could have hoped for it. He could have hoped only for such a resurrection as he described in his epistle to the Corinthians:

> "It is sown in corruption, it is raised in incorruption;....it is raised in glory;....it is raised in power;....it is raised a spiritual body. And as we have borne the image of the earthy, we shall also bear the image of the heavenly."

Having thus shown that the text furnishes no support to the doctrine which is brought forward to substantiate, we pass to its affirmative consideration, and to present what we believe to be its true meaning.

First of all, we should bear in mind that there are two kinds of resurrection spoken of in the Scriptures—just as there are two kinds of death, natural and moral death. As a state of sin is spoken of as a state of moral death, so a deliverance from that state is spoken of as a resurrection from that spiritual death; that is, a spiritual exaltation takes place. And as this moral death may be experienced during the natural life, so may this spiritual resurrection be also experienced during this life. Therefore, when we read in the Bible of "dead" and "death," we cannot determine simply from the use of these words that the writer designed to teach the absolute extinction of life; because these terms are employed in a figurative sense, as significant of moral death—as being dead in trespasses and in sin. So when we read in the Scriptures of a resurrection, it does not necessarily refer to the immortal resurrection of man; because there is a moral resurrection spoken of in the Bible, which may be experienced in this world—a spiritual quickening of the sinner and deliverance from dead works—morally elevating him—raising him to the true dignity of his nature and to the enjoyments of spiritual life. When we read of a resurrection, we should carefully peruse the context, to ascertain whether the writer refers to the immortal resurrection of man; or to a moral resurrection experienced by the true believer in passing from death unto life.

Dr. George Campbell, a learned divine of the orthodox school, in his "Notes" on the Four Gospels, vol. ii., p. 113, says that

> "The word *anastasin*, or rather the phrase *anastasis ton nekron*, is indeed the common term by which the resurrection, properly so called, is denominated in the New Testament. Yet, this is neither the only nor the primitive import of the word *anastasis;* it denotes simply being raised from inactivity to action, or from obscurity to eminence, or a return to such a state after an interruption. The verb *anistemi*, has the like latitude of signification; and both words are used in this extent by the writers of the New Testament, as well as by the LXX. Agreeably, therefore, to the original import, rising from a seat is properly termed *anastasis;* so in awaking out of sleep, or promotion from an inferior condition."

According to this learned divine, who should be regarded as good authority upon this subject, the original word, *anastasis*, translated resurrection, "is indeed the common term by which the resurrection" of man from the dead is denominated—yet he says that this is not the only, nor even the primitive import of the word. It denotes simply being raised from inactivity to action or promotion from an inferior condition. Hence, the mere use of the word in the scripture we are considering, furnishes no proof that it refers to the resurrection of all men—and as we have already shown that it does not refer to the immortal resurrection as described by scripture writers—hence it must have reference to a moral resurrection—a spiritual exaltation enjoyed by the true believer in this world. Such an application harmonizes with the context, and the primitive import of the word.

The context justifies the conclusion, that the phrase, resurrection of life, refers to the moral life which the Christian enjoys—to the spiritual enjoyment and peace consequent on belief, and a reception of Christian truth. At the 24th verse of the context, Jesus says, "He that heareth my word, [that is, my doctrine, my truth], and believeth on Him that sent me, hath everlasting life, and shall not come into condemnation; but is passed from death unto life." Those who believed not were in a state of moral death while in this world; the change wrought in them by belief and adoption of the truth, is spoken of as a resurrection; thus they pass from death unto life eternal, by being brought to the knowledge of God's truth. The believer was morally raised and elevated—spiritually exalted—enjoyed everlasting life—came forth to the resurrection of life—while the unbeliever was in a state of condemnation and death, or came forth to the resurrection of damnation.

Thus we see that those who believed on Christ, embraced his truth and religion, passed from death unto life. The death alluded to here, was not the death of the body, but death in sin. So the "life" spoken of was a state of mind opposite to death—the life which Christianity brings to the soul by an application of its spirit—spiritual life. The same life and death are referred to by the apostle Paul, in the following language: "And you hath he quickened, who were dead in trespasses and sins." (Eph. ii. 1). The wicked unbeliever is said to be dead in sin; while the true, Christian believer, is said to be alive unto God. The same idea is expressed in other phraseology,—"Awake, thou that sleepest, and arise from the dead, and Christ shall give thee light." (Eph. v. 14).

At the 25th verse of the context, we read thus: "Verily, verily, I say unto you, the hour is coming, and now is, when the dead [spiritually dead] shall hear the voice of the Son of God: and they that hear shall live."

The phrase "the dead," here, did not embrace all who were dead in sin, as we understand the expression, but such only as were soon to embrace Christian truth, and through its quickening power, pass from death unto life. This seems evident from the expression, "The hour is coming, and now is," referring to time and events then near at hand. Those only are referred to, who were to believe on Christ by attending on the personal ministration of his word, by receiving the truth from his own lips. Such were to hear the voice of the Son of God, and be convinced through his own personal labors and preaching. Many thus believed on him, (see John iv. 41, and other places), and lived the Christian life.

But few Jews, however, were disposed to receive him as the true Messiah—the Sent of God. They rejected him, would not honor him, and called him an imposter, and ridiculed the idea that God was with him, as he claimed, and had committed all judgment into his hands. The Jews thought it absurd in the extreme, that Jesus should claim to be the Son of God, and to have power to give life unto man! They were astonished that Jesus claimed to teach by divine authority—such a poor, unlettered, uninfluential person! Yet he claimed to have authority to execute judgment—to do God's will and to have power to give everlasting life to all who should believe on him as the Christ of God! This seemed to excite surprise in the minds of the Jews.

Marvel not at this—surprised though you are, I can tell you of more marvelous things than these, more astonishing things than I have yet told you! The hour is coming when all that are in their graves shall come forth; as much as to say, "you affect surprise that any shall believe on me and have life through a reception of my truth—you need not, for the time is coming, (he does not say, and now is, as before, for he knew the stubbornness of their hearts), when all that are in their graves shall hear his voice, that is, his doctrine, or word. Marvel as you do, surprised though you are, yet I will now tell you what will excite your astonishment still more—you, yourselves will yet come forth to the resurrection of moral life or death, or, in other words, the time is coming when you will see that I am the one to execute judgment, and you will all be judged according to the principles of my religion, and be acquitted or condemned."

As though Jesus had said, some on hearing my gospel will become my followers and have everlasting life—such will do a good thing by embracing my religion and shall be rewarded with spiritual life and true Christian enjoyment; while such as refuse my teachings and reject my religion and truth shall be condemned as guilty. The meaning seems to be this: The time was nigh at hand, when those dead in sin should be awakened from their lethargy, and be brought forth to judgment, and condemned by Christian principles.

The expression, "all that are in the graves," at the 28th verse, embraces a much larger number of the same class of individuals that are referred to in verse 25th, by the term "dead."

In the Scriptures, mankind are frequently represented as being dead, and sometimes as being in their graves. When a people are in a low state of sin and degradation, they are said to be dead, or in the "dust," or in their "graves." And when they rose out of that state of moral pollution, they were represented as rising from the dead, or coming forth from their graves, or out of the dust.

In the xxxvii. chap. of Ezekiel, the house of Israel is represented as being dead and in their graves, and their resurrection from the dead, is spoken of in the following language:

> "Therefore prophesy and say unto them, Thus saith the Lord God; Behold, O my people, I will open your graves, and cause you to come up out of your graves, and bring you into the land of Israel. And ye shall know that I am the Lord, when I have opened your graves, O my people, and brought you up out of your graves. And shall put my Spirit in you, and ye shall live, and I shall place you in your own land: then shall ye know that I the Lord have spoken it, and performed it, saith the Lord." Ezek. xxxvii. 12, 13, 14.

This has no reference to literal death or literal graves. In the passage under consideration the Jewish people are spoken of as being dead, and those who gave heed to the instructions of Christ, are represented as coming forth to the resurrection of life, though all that were in their "graves" should hear his voice. This language is not used here in a literal sense, but to represent their degraded condition. A state of sin was a state of death. "You hath he quickened who were dead in trespasses and in sin." The gospel quickened man into moral life; then he came forth, out of the dust of the earth—he passed from death into life.

We are sometimes told this interpretation of the Scriptures is forced and unnatural. But when there is not a particular theory to defend, other religionists than ourselves put the same construction upon similar language. In one of the hymns of Dr. Watts, we find the following verse, which candid people find no difficulty in understanding. They place the same construction upon it that we do upon similar phraseology when found in the Scriptures. The verse reads as follows:

"But where the Gospel comes,
It sheds diviner light,
It calls *dead* sinners from their *tombs*,
And gives the blind their sight."

The hymn containing this verse is sung in all the pulpits of the land. Thus, "sinners" are represented as being dead and in their tombs! The divine light of the Gospel "calls these dead sinners from their tombs, and gives the blind their sight." Here sinners are represented as coming forth from their "tombs"—the same as they are in the Scriptures as coming forth from their graves. It represents simply, in both cases, the moral influence of divine truth upon the soul. The gospel of Christ "calls dead sinners from their tombs," and bringing them out of their "tombs," or "graves," they come forth to a resurrection of life, joy, and peace, and hence are in possession of everlasting life.

The resurrection of life means the spiritual life which the Christian enjoys—the reward consequent on a reception of the truth—such as embraced Jesus' religion passed from death unto life. The same idea is expressed in the exhortation of the apostle: "Awake, thou that sleepest, and rise from the dead, and Christ shall give thee light."

Those who should come forth to damnation, would be aroused from their state of ignorance and sin, and stand forth condemned for rejecting Christian truth. They would not awake till they had filled up the measure of their iniquity; then it would be too late to save them from a merited retribution. Though they should suffer punishment for their sin, yet they should finally be redeemed, for all Israel shall be saved. Rom. xi. 20–32.

# YE SHALL ALL LIKEWISE PERISH.

"But except ye repent, ye shall all likewise perish."—LUKE xiii. 3.

Many have erroneously supposed that this Scripture referred to the future, immortal state of existence, and taught the doctrine of endless suffering for a large portion of the intelligent creation. And this is the popular sentiment of the professed Christian church at the present day—though some learned orthodox divines have given to the passage a different explanation.

In times of sectarian revivals—falsely called "religious excitements"—those to be wrought upon by frightful descriptions of hell and of the agony of lost souls, are informed that if they repent not at once, perhaps before the sun shall rise again, they may be suffering in hell, all the agonies of the second death, and that they may be plunged headlong beneath the rolling billows of the fiery sea of hell, and be tormented by fiends as long as the throne of the Eternal God shall stand!

But instead of this text having reference to the immortal world, the immediate context plainly shows that it has reference to scenes and events connected with this life. No allusion is made in the context to the resurrection state; it does not say that if the sinner does not repent in time, that he shall be made miserable to all eternity. The context does not furnish the slightest justification for such an assertion.

At the commencement of the chapter, we are informed that there were present with the Savior "some who told him of the Galileans, whose blood Pilate had mingled with their sacrifices." This does not mean that blood was mingled with the sacrifices offered, but while the Galileans were offering sacrifices, they were slain by the authority of Pilate; and hence their blood being poured out around the sacrificial altar, it was said to be "mingled with their sacrifices."

It seems that the Jews looked upon this destruction of the Galileans, as coming upon them on account of their great guilt and iniquity. Hence, Jesus said, "Suppose ye that these Galileans were sinners above all the Galileans, because they suffered such things?" There is no proof of this. "I tell you, nay; but except ye repent, ye shall all likewise perish;" or, ye shall perish in like manner, or in a way somewhat similar. As though Jesus had said, "You refer me to some who perished around the altar while offering sacrifice; this you regard as a judgment of God upon their sins; but they were not sinners above all men, because such was their fate. You are equally guilty yourselves; and now I say to you, that unless you turn from your iniquity, you will, ere long meet with a similar fate; if you go on, you will soon fill up the measure of your iniquity, and perish in like manner."

Here a comparison is instituted between the fate of the Galileans and the fate of the Jews addressed, in case they repented not. "Except ye repent, ye shall all likewise perish." Like whom? we would ask. Ans. Like those Galileans referred to; or, like those eighteen mentioned in the 4th verse, "upon whom the tower of Siloam fell and slew them, think ye that they were sinners above all men that dwell in Jerusalem? I tell you, nay; but except ye repent, ye shall all likewise perish;" or, in a similar way.

How did those referred to perish? Ans. By temporal judgments — they were slain by the sword, around the altar — or, by the falling of the tower in Siloam; the Jews, if they repented not, should perish in like manner, or in a similar way.

It is not said that they should perish like some who had been hurled down to endless woe, by the arm of the Almighty; but they should perish like those upon whom the tower in Siloam fell and slew them; i. e., in a similar way—by severe temporal calamities and judgments. There would be a striking similarity between the destruction of the Galileans and the destruction of those to whom Jesus refers. When victorious armies should come upon them, they would be slain about the temple and their blood even would be mingled with their sacrifices.

Josephus informs us that when Jerusalem was beseiged by the Romans, hundreds were slain in and about the temple. He says:

"Now round about the altars lay dead bodies heaped one upon another, as at the steps going up to it, ran a great quantity of blood, whither also the dead bodies that were slain above (on the altar) fell down.....One would have thought that the hill itself, on which the temple stood, was seething hot, as full of fire on every part of it, that the blood was larger in quantity than the fire, and those that were slain more in number than those that slew them; for the ground did nowhere appear visible, for the dead bodies that lay on it."—*Book VI.*, Chaps. IV., V.

Many Orthodox divines have given the text a similar construction. Dr. Adam Clarke comments thus:

"Ye shall all likewise perish. In a like way, in the same manner. This prediction of our Lord was literally fulfilled. When the city was taken by the Romans, multitudes of the priests, etc., *who were going on with their sacrifices*, were slain, and their blood mingled with the blood of their victims; and multitudes were buried under the ruins of the walls, houses and temple."

Dr. Barnes, an eminent Presbyterian divine, says thus:

"You shall all be destroyed in a *similar manner*......This was remarkably fulfilled. Many of the Jews were slain in the temple; many while offering sacrifice; thousands perished in a way very similar to the Galileans."

CALMET.—"Jesus Christ here predicts those calamities which overwhelmed them, when Jerusalem was destroyed by the Romans; for then, very many impenitent and unbelieving Jews were buried together under the ruins of their most miserable nation."

PEARCE.—"Except ye, the nation of the Jews, repent, your state shall be destroyed."

WHITBY.—"I tell you, nay; but except ye repent, ye shall all likewise perish, for the same cause, and many of you after the same manner."

# THE DAMNATION OF UNBELIEF.

"He that believeth and is baptized, shall be saved; but he that believeth not, shall be damned."—MARK xvi. 16.

THIS passage is regarded as one of the strongest proof texts of the doctrine of endless punishment that is found in the sacred Scriptures. It is supposed to have reference to the immortal state of existence and to teach the endless ruin of all who die in unbelief. Those who believe, in this life, and are baptized, it is said, will be saved from hell in the life to come; while those who believe not in this world, will be made miserable in the world to come. But the attentive reader will bear in mind that such an interpretation is entirely unsupported by the text. It is assumed. The passage makes no allusion to the immortal condition of mankind. The common exposition of the subject involves its advocates in inexplicable difficulties. It is supposed that water baptism is alluded to in this passage. If so, some particular mode of baptism is referred to; but how are we to determine what mode of baptism is taught? We are not instructed upon this point, and professed Christians entertain quite dissimilar views upon this subject; some contend that immersion is the only mode taught in the Bible, while others contend for sprinkling and pouring and plunging. If water baptism be essential to salvation, then it must be administered in some prescribed form. In absence of all proof upon this point, how are we to determine what form to employ?

Again: if belief be absolutely essential to secure immortal felicity, then a true faith is necessary; for to assert that belief is an indispensable requisite to reach the heavenly kingdom, and then affirm that it is unimportant what kind of belief a man embraces, is the height of folly! If man's eternal salvation depend upon faith in this life, where, amidst the conflicting theories in Christendom, will he go for salvation? Each sect claims to have the true faith, how then can we determine which belief to accept and which to reject?

Again: the exposition of the text which has extensively obtained, sweeps the whole intelligent universe of God down to perdition —for all men have been unbelievers—and the language is positive — he that believeth not SHALL be damned. If all are to be excluded from heaven who believe not, then infants and idiots and the whole heathen world must be lost forever. The heathen have not heard of Christ, and how could they believe on him of whom they have not heard? Are millions on millions of human beings to be hurled down to perdition for not believing on Christ, when they have not even heard of Christ?

Again: if we give to the text a universal application, then there are no true believers on earth at the present time, for there is not a single human being that can produce the signs which were to follow believers!

"And these signs shall follow them that believe: In my name shall they cast out devils; they shall speak with new tongues; they shall take up serpents, and if they drink any deadly thing it shall not hurt them; they shall lay hands on the sick, and they shall recover." Mark xvi. 17, 18.

Now, where, in this age of the world, shall we look for believers, according to this test? Who can produce the signs? Where is the Christian believer who can cast out devils? or can speak with new tongues; or play with the fangs of the serpent and not be bitten;

or drink the poisonous draught and not be injured? Where is the believer now who can heal the sick, restore sight to the blind, and hearing to the deaf? "These signs shall follow them that believe. They shall take up serpents, and if they drink any deadly thing it shall not hurt them; they shall lay hands on the sick and they shall recover." As believers in Christ cannot now produce the signs here indicated, we conclude that the subject cannot have a universal application. From the signs which were to follow believers, it is evident that the text had special reference to the disciples of our Lord, who were commissioned to preach the gospel of his kingdom, and establish the truths connected with his dispensation of grace.

As the apostles alone could exhibit the signs here designated, the subject had exclusive reference to the apostolic age. Jesus selected a few disciples to be his companions and co-laborers, to participate in the enjoyments of his religion, and share the perils of his mission. They had toiled together, endured the scorn of the proud and haughty Pharisee, and the buffetings and contumely of the world. He had imparted instruction concerning the principles of his kingdom, though they did not fully comprehend the character of his religion, nor the nature and extent of his mission.

Jesus had spoken of the direful judgments and severe national calamities which were soon to come upon that disobedient and sinful people, which would sweep them down to destruction. He had told them of his crucifixion, and that he would rise again from the dead; but his disciples did not fully appreciate the nature of his work; and when he was seized by his enemies and put to death, they gave up in despair. They had no expectation of meeting their Lord and Master again! Heavy of heart and full of sorrow, the disciples were convened together to bemoan their fate, and weep together that their Master had been taken from them, and with wicked hands had been crucified and slain. While in this dejected state of mind, hope having expired in their bosoms, the tidings came to them that Jesus had risen, but the information seemed to them improbable, and the historian tells us that they "mourned and wept and believed not."

Those disciples were unbelieving, and Jesus appeared unto them, the context informs us, as they sat at meat, and upbraided them for their unbelief and hardness of heart, because they believed not them that had seen him, after he had risen. The disciples were here called unbelievers — they believed not for joy. But the evidence was overwhelming, that their Master had risen from the dead; and there they were commissioned to go forth and preach the gospel to every creature. He that believeth — or, those of you who believe in me as a true Teacher sent from God, shall be saved, and those who believe not shall be damned, or condemned. The Greek word (*katakrino*) which is here rendered *damned*, occurs in several other passages, though it is translated "damned" in but one other text, Romans xiv. 23. "He that doubteth is damned." It is rendered *condemn*, and *condemned*, and *condemneth*. When a man doubts, he is damned; *or* in a state of condemnation.

Macknight in this passage renders the original, "condemned." Dr. Campbell, another orthodox divine, says that the original word rendered "damned" corresponds exactly to the English verb "condemn." The same word occurs in Matt. xx. 18, and is applied to Christ: "They shall condemn him to death." No one supposes that this refers to misery in the future world, and yet it is the same word as occurs in the text and is rendered damned! It occurs again Matt. xxvii. 3:

"Then Judas, who had betrayed him (Jesus) when he saw that he was condemned (*katakrino*) repented himself," etc. It is found also in John viii. 10, where Jesus said to the guilty woman: "Hath no man condemned (*katakrino*) thee?—neither do I condemn thee." "They all condemned (*katakrino*) him (Christ) to be guilty of death." Mark xiv. 64.

No one supposes that these passages allude to misery in the immortal world. Neither does the text refer to the immortal condition of man. The risen Lord commissioned his apostles to preach the gospel, or good news that he had risen from the dead, and was conqueror of hell and of death. Those thus sent out were endowed with miraculous powers—certain signs should follow them. The succeeding context informs us, that they went forth and preached everywhere, the Lord working with them, and confirming the word with signs following. Mark xvi. 20.

The disciples went forth proclaiming the gospel, or good news that their Lord had risen from the dead; that he was conqueror of hell and of death, and was alive again forevermore. They were baptized with the Holy Ghost and with fire, and gave evidence of their divine commission by the signs following them. For a specific purpose, miraculous powers were given unto them, so that the sick were restored, the blind made to see, the lame to walk, the insane clothed in their right minds, and hope was kindled in the hearts of those who were filled with despair.

Those believing disciples were saved from moral darkness and blindness of mind, from erroneous views of the character and government of God; from the fear which has torment, and from the impending judgments which came upon that sinful people, who turned from the divine instructions of Jesus and cruelly put him to death. In believing on Christ, they entered into rest and had joy that was unspeakable and full of glory. The text had special application to the disciples of our Lord. We have already seen how full of doubt they were, when their Master was crucified, and that Jesus had occasion to reprove them for their unbelief, and upbraid them for their hardness of heart. But on being convinced of the resurrection of Jesus, they went forth on their divine mission, proclaiming the truth, the Lord confirming the word with signs following. They could produce the signs which were to follow those who believed. This passage, therefore, had special reference to the primitive Christians, who could produce the "signs" specified in the context, which were to follow believers. The text evidently was originally designed to be restricted in its application to those early Christians who were endowed with miraculous power, and, therefore, we cannot give to it a general or universal application.

# EVERLASTING CONTEMPT.

"And many of them that sleep in the dust of the earth shall awake, some to everlasting life and some to shame *and* everlasting contempt."—DAN. xii. 2.

As many have erroneously supposed that this passage refers to the immortal condition of the whole human race, and describes the future happiness and misery of different classes of individuals, after the resurrection of all mankind from the dead, we ask the careful attention of the reader to the considerations we are about to present.

First, such an interpretation of this text is assumed to be correct, as the passage itself furnishes no proof of its correctness. Not the least hint is given of the immortal state of existence. No allusion is made to the resurrection of man from the dead. The passage does not assert that many shall "awake" in the future world; this is taken for granted. The very thing is assumed which needs undoubted proof! If the passage is to be understood literally, we may as well assume that those who awake from the dust of the earth, will awake into this world as into the future state. In absence of all proof, we certainly have no right to assume that the text refers to the immortal, resurrection world.

Again: It is supposed that the text refers to the time when the whole human race will be raised from the dead, and to a day of general judgment after that event; and yet orthodoxy teaches that the condition of every soul is unalterably fixed at death, and that all men are either in a state of happiness or misery! If all have a conscious existence in heaven or hell immediately after death, as orthodoxy teaches, in what sense do all sleep in the dust of the earth? All are to awake from the dust of the earth and come forth to judgment, to rise either to everlasting life or everlasting shame and contempt, and yet it is earnestly contended that all are in a state of happiness or misery at death! Orthodoxy teaches that long *before* the judgment day, the righteous are enjoying everlasting life, and the wicked suffering everlasting shame and contempt, and yet, at that day, they will awake from the dust of the earth and come to judgment, when long before they have been *judged*, acquitted or condemned, according to their merits or demerits.

These considerations show the fallacy of the orthodox interpretation of the passage before us; and we therefore seek an exposition of the text which will be more rational and scriptural.

We shall be essentially assisted in our investigation of the subject before us, by ascertaining the ancient mode of speech, and the meaning of peculiar expressions employed by the ancients to convey important truths. When people were in a low and humble condition, they were spoken of as being bowed in the dust, and dwelling in the dust. These expressions were employed to represent a state of subjection, degradation, and humiliation.

Cruden says that "dust" signifies not simply grave and death, but "a most low and miserable condition." 1 Sam. ii. 8, God raiseth up the poor out of the dust. Nahum iii. 18, Thy nobles shall dwell in the dust: "*They shall be reduced to a mean condition.*"

Speaking of Solomon, David says that "his enemies shall lick the dust." Ps. lxxii. 9. The meaning of this is, as Dr. Clarke says, that his enemies shall become so completely subdued, that they shall be reduced to the most abject state of vassalage; hence, they were said to lick the dust.

Again, we read: "For He bringeth down them that dwell on high; the lofty city, He layeth it low; He layeth it low, even to the ground; He bringeth it *even to the dust.*" Isa. xxvi. 5. This being brought "to the dust" was a figurative expression to denote a low and abject condition. Hence, when Job wanted to humble himself, he speaks of himself as repenting "in dust and ashes." Job xlii. 6. So by a figure of speech, by repentance, he would rise from the dust; that is, be delivered from that distressed and humble condition. When the divine judgments came upon Ariel, or Jerusalem, that city is represented as being low in the dust. "And thou shalt be brought down, and shalt speak *out of the ground*, and thy speech shall be *low out of the dust.*" Isa. xxix. 4.

We thus see that a low and abject condition was spoken of by representing people to be "in the dust;" so, on the other hand, a deliverance from that condition was spoken of as rising from the dust, and shaking thyself from the dust, and even awaking from the dust. "AWAKE and sing, ye that DWELL IN THE DUST." Isa. xxvi. 19. Those who had been brought down to the dust, (see verse 5th of this chapter,) were commanded to "awake" and sing; that is, they were to awake out of the dust.

Jerusalem was exhorted to *awake* from the dust, thus:

"Awake, awake; put on thy strength, O Zion; put on thy beautiful garments, O Jerusalem, the holy city: for henceforth there shall no more come unto thee the uncircumcised and the unclean. SHAKE THYSELF FROM THE DUST; ARISE, and sit down, O Jerusalem," etc. Isa. lii. 1, 2.

Here Jerusalem is exhorted to *awake* and *arise* and shake herself from the dust! The people were to be raised from an humble and degraded condition to a state of prosperity. Hence, God is said to raise the poor "out of the dust," (Ps. cxiii. 7,) that is, from an abject condition to a state of happiness, to the enjoyment of favors and privileges of which they had been deprived. Dr. Clarke says that "He may allude to the wretched state of the captives in Babylon, whom God raised up out of that dust and dunghill." See also 1 Sam. ii. 8; 1 Kings xvi. 2.

To be in the "dust of the earth" was to be in a low and degraded condition, and to rise from it, was to be in a state of prosperity.

But the passage under consideration speaks of *sleeping in the dust of the earth.* Every reader of the Bible is aware that the term "sleep" is used in different senses in the Scriptures. It is conceded by all that it is used to represent the extinction of animal life—a state we call death. John xi. 12, 13; 1

Cor. xv. 51. It is also employed to represent a state of slothfulness and poverty. See Prov. vi. 9–11, and xxiv. 33, 34. It is also employed to set forth a state of moral and spiritual death. Isa. xxix. 10; 1 Tim. v. 6; Rev. iii. 1. We learn by these passages that people were represented as being dead and asleep while in this state of existence. They were morally dead and spiritually asleep; hence, when they were delivered from this state, they were spoken of as rising from the dead and awaking out of sleep, and even out of the *dust* of the earth. "Awake, thou that sleepest, and *arise from the dead,* and Christ shall give thee light." Eph. v. 14. Those here referred to and called upon to *awake* from sleep, were in a state of moral and spiritual death—and to arise from the dead, here, was the same as to awake from the dust of the earth. Such were exhorted to "*awake to righteousness* and sin not." 1 Cor. xv. 34. We have already seen that similar phraseology was employed to represent the moral and spiritual condition of nations. Babylon is spoken of as being "in the dust." Isa. xlvii. 1. And Jerusalem was exhorted to awake and shake herself from the dust. Isa. lii. 2. Then the people rose out of a low and degraded condition.

Reference is made in the text to the Jewish people. They had once enjoyed great privileges and favors as the chosen people of God. They had been a powerful nation, and exerted a commanding influence among the nations of the earth. But they became a proud, haughty, and disobedient people, and were ultimately brought into a low and degraded condition, lost their national power and influence, and experienced the retributive justice of God. The text under consideration alluded to the time when severe national judgments would come upon the Jewish nation, and some would awake to an appreciation of the truth and believe on Christ, and acknowledge him before men, while others would secretly believe on him but publicly deny him, and such would awake to shame and everlasting contempt.

"And many of them that sleep in the dust of the earth shall awake." Many who were in a low and degraded condition should be aroused from their lethargy—"some to everlasting life;" that is, to an appreciation of the truth, and the Savior's claims, and would believe on him and *have* everlasting life—while others would secretly accept him, but not having sufficient moral courage to avow their convictions, would awake to "shame and everlasting contempt." Those who boldly confessed Christ as their Lord and Master, awoke to "everlasting life," while those who were convinced in their own souls that he was a true teacher sent from God, but were too timid to make a public avowal of their convictions, and thus practically gave their influence against him, "awoke to shame and everlasting contempt." We read that "among the chief rulers, also, MANY believed on him, but because of the Pharisees *they did not confess him*, lest they should be put out of the synagogue. For they loved the praise of men more than the praise of God." John xii. 42, 43.

Here we are distinctly informed that many, among even the chief rulers, believed on Christ, were convinced in their souls that Christ was divinely commissioned, but locked up their convictions in the secret chambers of their hearts, and dare not make a profession of their faith, through fear of the opposition and persecution which they would encounter. "Many" thus awoke from their slumber, in the dust of the earth, to shame and contempt! They were ashamed to be true to the honest convictions of their souls, ashamed to own Christ before men, ashamed to acknowledge him as their Master, and he was ashamed to own such as his disciples. See Mark viii. 38; Luke xii. 8, 9. "Many" believed on Christ, but were ashamed to own him publicly. Such "awoke" to an appreciation of the truth, but *awoke to shame and everlasting contempt.* Their conduct merited the shame and contempt that were visited upon them. Those who were true to their convictions, and publicly espoused their faith in Christ, in face of persecution and danger, awoke to everlasting life, and were "not ashamed of the gospel of Christ," for they were animated with a hope that maketh not ashamed. "Some shall awake to shame and everlasting contempt." Some believed on him, but could not endure persecution, and turned back again to the enemy, and suffered in the divine judgments which came upon the ungodly, and when they awoke to a realizing sense of their condition, and cried, "Lord, Lord, open unto us;" it was then too late to escape the punishment they deserved, and they awoke to shame and everlasting contempt. They had known the truth, had secretly believed on Christ, but had been ashamed to own him before men, and now they must suffer the divine judgments "in that time of trouble, such as never was since there was a nation, even to that same time."

Dan. xii. 1. Or, as Matthew has it, "great tribulation, such as was not since the beginning of the world, to this time, no, nor ever shall be." Matt. xxiv. 21. This was the abomination of desolation spoken of by Daniel, the prophet. Matt. xxiv. 15; Dan. xii. 1–11. And all things spoken of were to be fulfilled in that generation. Matt. xxiv. 34. Those who believed in Christ and confessed him before men, were in possession of everlasting life, while those who believed in him, but stifled their convictions, and denied him before men, and joined hands with his enemies, awoke to shame and everlasting contempt! They had been ashamed to confess him publicly, and they awoke to realize the shame and contempt they merited and experienced!

# THE STRAIT GATE.

"Enter ye in at the strait gate: for wide is the gate and broad is the way that leadeth to destruction: and many there be which go in thereat; Because strait is the gate, and narrow is the way which leadeth unto life, and few there be that find it."—MATT. vii. 13, 14.

THAT we may readily apprehend the meaning of this passage, we must consider its relation to the immediate context, and give to it an interpretation which will harmonize with the character and perfections of our heavenly Father, and the just and beneficent principles of his moral government. Many have erred in attempting to bring the Divine Being down to their mistaken and unworthy ideas, and making Him conform to their theological opinions, instead of bringing their own sentiments into harmony with the charter and perfections of God. Hence an interpretation has been given to the passage before us, opposed to the nature of God, and the teachings of his word.

It is believed that all men, being born totally depraved, with corrupt natures, are in the broad road to destruction, which leads to endless pain and wretchedness, and that millions on millions of God's intelligent offspring will be endlessly destroyed. They will suffer, as Dr. Watts expresses it, amidst

"Eternal plagues and heavy chains,
Tormenting racks and fiery coals."

But such opinions are opposed to the teachings of nature and revelation, and we dismiss them as unworthy of our regard.

What then is meant, we pass now to inquire, by "Entering into the strait gate?" The context shows that Jesus had reference to those moral obligations and duties, which grow out of our relation to kindred humanity and which are enjoined upon us, because of our relationship to each other. God being the common Father of all, consequently we are members of one great family, hence, there are relative duties growing out of this relationship, the discharge of which, constitutes us characteristically, children of God, and true and faithful disciples of his Son. Jesus was imparting that moral instruction designed to enlighten man in regard to his duties and obligations, both towards God and kindred humanity. He would send him to search his own heart and detect the passions lurking there; enter into a thorough exami nation of himself, and not overlook his own imperfections and wrongs, in searching for the sins of others.

As the moral obligations and duties thus imposed upon man were so numerous, instead of individual specifications, Jesus sums them up in the following broad and comprehensive language: "Therefore, ALL things, whatsoever ye would that men should do to you, do ye even so to them; for this is the law and the prophets." And then he adds immediately: "Enter ye in at *the* strait gate," or, enter ye in at *this* strait gate of doing to others, as ye would that they should do unto you. By the "strait gate," and "narrow way which leadeth unto life," we understand that reference is made to that course of moral excellence and Christian principle, and integrity, which the gospel recognizes, and which leadeth unto life. Such, animated by a divine spirit, are spoken of as being in the "kingdom of God," which consists in "righteousness, peace and joy in the holy spirit." Such were in possession of "everlasting life."

It was only by complying with the requisitions of Christ, and doing to others as he would be done by, that man could become a Christian and enter into life. And as few only, made practical the Savior's teachings, hence, it was said, "few there be that find it." As the masses were governed by opposite principles, which lead to retaliation and revenge, it was appropriately said: "Broad is the way which leadeth to destruction, and many there be which go in thereat." Those who were regardless of moral principles, were in the broad road to destruction. They were in the way of sin and death, while those who gave heed to the Savior's teachings were in the narrow way of life and peace.

The Psalmist says: "Open to me the gates of righteousness, I will praise the Lord. This gate of the Lord, into which the righteous shall enter." When a man begins to live the Christian life, then doth he enter the gate of righteousness; and through this gate of righteousness, or right doing, does he enter into the kingdom of God, which consists in righteousness, peace and joy in the holy spirit. And so small was the number comparatively, who entered the gate of righteousness, by doing as they would be done by, that it was said, "few there be that find it." He is in the way of life that keepeth instruction. Those who gave heed to the instructions of Jesus were in the way of life —they were in possession of everlasting life,

Christ said: "The words that I speak unto you, they are spirit, and they are life," and those who kept his words were in the way of life, for "he that hath the Son, hath life."

In this enlightened and Christian age of the world, how few enter this gate of righteousness, and walk in this narrow way of doing to others in all things as they would that others should do unto them. In this material age, when so many bow at the shrine of mammon, when there is such a fearful rush for gold, for honor, and fame, and office, how few there are who find this narrow way? Alas! how many rush into the broad road of sin and death!

"Broad is the way which leadeth to destruction." This language has no reference to the future immortal world, but refers simply to the destructive power of sin in this life. He who is in the way of sin is in the way of destruction. Paul, speaking of the Jew and Gentile, says: "they have all gone out of the way....Destruction and misery are in their ways." And so destruction and misery are in the way of every sinner. The way of the transgressor is hard, we should therefore, flee from sin and walk in the way of life — this strait and narrow way which leadeth unto life, and shineth more and more, even unto the perfect day. All are called away from the broad road of sin and destruction. Sin mars the moral image of God, and is destructive to man's peace and happiness, we should, therefore, flee from it as from a pestilence.

What we need is simply to make Christianity practical, to enter this strait gate, and walk in this narrow way of doing to others in all things, as we would that they should do unto us. Then shall we be in the way of life, of peace and salvation.

# THE CASE OF JUDAS.

"It had been good for that man if he had not been born."—MATT. xxvi. 24.

THESE words are supposed, by many professed religionists, to teach the endless perdition of Judas. How could it have been said of Judas, it is asked, "It had been good for that man if he had not been born," if he is finally to be saved? If he is to reach heaven at last, it certainly was good for him to have been born.

Many erroneous ideas have arisen in regard to the meaning of this passage by supposing that it had reference to the condition of Judas in the immortal state of existence. This language had not the least reference to the final condition of Judas. It was a common proverb among the Jews in our Savior's day, to indicate any severe calamity to befall an individual, without any reference to the future world. It had special application to events connected with this life. When any fearful calamity or judgment was to come upon an individual, it was common to say,

"It were good for that man if he had not been born." It was a proverbial expression, or an expression in common use among the Jews, to denote any severe chastisement or great misfortune, or terrible calamity. The Savior, knowing its use, and aware of the fate of Judas, very appropriately applied it to him. Similar expressions had long been in use. Job cursed the day of his birth, and said: "Let the day perish wherein I was born." Job iii. 1–3. Solomon said: "If a man live many years, and his soul be not filled with good; and also that he hath no burial: I say that an untimely birth is better than he." Eccles. vi. 3. This is the same as saying, "It had been better if he had not been born." It was a common proverb to denote any great misfortune coming upon an individual; and as Judas would be overwhelmed with sorrow and smitten with grief and anguish, plunged into the greatest distress by a vivid sense of his sins, it was very properly applied to him without any reference to his immortal condition.

Kenrick says, in his Exposition, the expression—

"'It had been good for him, if he had never been born,' is a *proverbial* phrase, and not to be understood literally: for it is not consistent with our ideas of the divine goodness to make the existence of any being a curse to him, or to cause him to suffer more, upon the whole, than he enjoys happiness. Rather than do this, God would not have created him at all. But as it is usual to say of men who are to endure some grievous punishment or dreadful calamity, that it would have been better for them never to have been born, Christ foreseeing what Judas would bring upon himself, by delivering up his Master into the hands of his enemies, applies this language to him."

We call the reader's attention to the following from Dr. Adam Clarke, the Methodist commentator, upon this subject. He enters into a labored argument to show that Judas may be saved, and that his repentance was sincere, genuine, and acceptable to God. After mature deliberation, he thinks that "there is no positive proof of the final damnation of Judas in the sacred text." This is the opinion of one of the most learned and distinguished divines of the orthodox church. Dr. Clarke shows clearly that the language that stands at the head of this article was a proverbial expression to denote the state of any flagrant transgressor without regard to the future world. But we will let this distinguished commentator speak for himself. He says:

"Judas was indisputably a bad man; but he might have been worse: we may plainly see that there were depths of wickedness to which he might have proceeded, and which were prevented by his repentance. Thus things appear to stand previously to his end. But is there any room for hope in his death? In answer to this, it must be understood,—first: That there is presumptive evidence that he did not destroy himself; and, second: That his repentance was sincere. If so, was it not possible for the mercy of God to extend even to his case? It did so to the murderers of the Son of God; and they were certainly worse men, (strange as this assertion may appear), than Judas. Even he gave them the fullest proof of Christ's innocence: their buying the field with the money Judas threw down, was the full proof of it; and yet, with every convincing evidence before them, they crucified our Lord. They excited Judas to betray his Master, and crucified him when they got him into their power, and therefore St. Stephen calls them both the betrayers and murderers of that Just One, (Acts vii. 52), in these respects they were more deeply criminal than Judas himself; yet, even to these very betrayers and murderers, Peter preaches repentance, with the promise of remission of sins, and the gift of the Holy Ghost. (Acts iii. 12–26). If, then, these were within the reach of mercy, and we are informed that a great company of the priests became obedient to the faith, (Acts vi. 7), then certainly Judas was not in such a state as precluded the possibility of his salvation. Surely the blood of the covenant could wash out even his stain, as it did that more deeply ingrained one, of the other betrayers and murderers of the Lord Jesus.

Should the 25th verse be urged against this possibility, because it is there said that Judas fell from his ministry and apostleship, that he might go to his own place, and that this place is hell. I answer,—first: It remains to be proved that this place means hell; and, second: It is not clear that the words are spoken of Judas at all, but of Matthias: his own place meaning that vacancy in the apostolate, to which he was then elected.

To say the repentance of Judas was merely the effect of his horror; that it did not spring from the compunction of heart; that it was legal and not evangelical, etc., is saying what none can with propriety say but God himself, who searches the heart. What renders his case most desperate, are the words of our Lord. (Matt. xxvi. 24). "Wo unto that man by whom the Son of Man is betrayed! It had been good for that man if he had not been born!" I have considered this saying in a general point of view in my note on Matt. xxvi. 24, and were it not a proverbial form of speech among the Jews to express the state of any flagrant transgressor, I should be led to apply it, in all its literal import, to the case of Judas, as I have done in the above note, in the case of any damned soul;

but when I find that it was a proverbial saying, and that it has been used in many cases, where the fixing of the irreversible doom of a sinner is not implied, it may be capable of a more favorable interpretation than what is generally given to it. I shall produce a few of those examples from Schoettgen, to which I have referred in my note on Matt. xxvi. 24.

In Chagigah, fol. 2, 2, it is said, 'Whoever considers these four things, it would have been better for him had he never come into the world, viz.: That which is above; that which is below; that which is before; and that which is behind. And whosoever does not attend to the honor of his Creator, it were better for him had he never been born.'

In Shemoth Rabba, sect. 40, fol. 135, 1, 2, it is said, 'Whosoever knows the law, and does not do it, it had been better for him had he never come into the world.'

In Vayikra Rabba, sect. 26, fol. 179, 4, and Midrash Coheleth, fol. 91, 4, it is thus expressed; 'It were better for him had he never been created; and it would have been better for him had he been strangled in the womb, and never have seen the light of this world.'

In Sohar Genes, fol. 71, col. 282, it is said, 'If any man be parsimonious towards the poor, it had been better for him had he never come into the world.' *Ibid*, fol. 84, col. 333. 'If any performs the law, not for the sake of the law, it were good for that man had he never been created.'

These examples sufficiently prove that this was a common proverb, and is used with a great variety and latitude of meaning; and seems intended to show that the case of such and such persons was not only very deplorable, but extremely dangerous; but does not imply the positive impossibility either of their repentance or salvation.

The utmost that can be said for the case of Judas is this: he committed a heinous act of sin and ingratitude; but he repented, and did what he could to undo his wicked act: he had committed the sin unto death, i. e., a sin that involves the death of the body; but who can say, (if mercy was offered to Christ's murderers, and the gospel was first to be preached at Jerusalem, that these very murderers might have the first offer of salvation through him whom they had pierced), that the same mercy could not be extended to wretched Judas? I contend, that the chief priests, etc., who instigated Judas to deliver up his Master, and who crucified him—and who crucified him, too, as a malefactor, having at the same time, the most indubitable evidence of his innocence—were worse men than Judas Iscariot himself; and that if mercy was extended to those, the wretched penitent traitor did not die out of the reach of the yearning of its bowels. And I contend farther, that there is no positive evidence of the final damnation of Judas in the sacred text.'—*Clarke in loco.*

This learned commentator contends that the repentance of Judas was genuine, and that "there is no positive evidence of the final damnation of Judas in the sacred text." Why, then, are we gravely asked, did he go and *hang* himself, as Matthew affirms? (Matt. xxvii. 5) We would here state, that Luke gives a somewhat different account of his death. See Acts i. 18: "And falling headlong, he *burst asunder in the midst*, and all his bowels gushed out." How, then, are we to reconcile this apparent discrepancy between the two evangelists? One affirms that he hanged himself, the other that he fell headlong and burst asunder. The difficulty in question arises from an incorrect translation of the Greek word *apegzato*, here rendered "hanged himself." It does not necessarily have this meaning, and may be rendered, "was suffocated, as with grief or anguish." Eminent critics, as Dr. Clarke says, believe that Judas was suffocated with excessive grief. "Wakefield (he adds), supports this meaning of the word with great learning and ingenuity." Dr. George Campbell, an eminent Scotch Presbyterian divine, says that "the Greek word plainly denotes *strangling*, but does not say how, by hanging, or otherwise. It is quite a different term that is used in those places where hanging is mentioned." He also adds, that it may be rendered, "was suffocated." Wakefield renders it, "was choked with anguish." This rendering of the original is supported by high authority, and is evidently correct.

Judas was overwhelmed with a sense of his sin, and sincerely repented before God, carried back the ill-gotten gain, and died of excessive grief, "was chocked with anguish," or "was suffocated." His grief was most intense; his anguish so burdensome, that he reeled beneath the oppressive load of guilt and sorrow, and fell prostrate to the earth, being suffocated with grief. He gave every evidence possible of deep sorrow for sin, and of genuine repentance.

# SIN UNTO DEATH.

"If a man see his brother sin a sin *which is* not unto death, he shall ask, and he shall give him life for them that sin unto death. There is a sin unto death: I do not say that he shall pray for it. All unrighteousness is sin: and there is a sin not unto death."—1 JOHN v. 16, 17.

THIS passage has been sadly misinterpreted, not only by many honest and sincere Christians, but its meaning has not always been apparent to some learned theologians. Some have supposed that it referred to what is called the "unpardonable sin," for the forgiveness of which we should not pray. But some of the most eminent commentators admit that the apostle here made no reference to the sin against the Holy Ghost. "I do not think," says Adam Clarke, "the passage has anything to do with what is termed *the sin against the Holy Ghost*, which I have proved no man can now commit." The evident design of the apostle was to cultivate a heavenly disposition and temper in his brethren, and a tender spirit toward the erring. Under the Jewish law some sins were punishable with death, and those who committed offences, the penalty of which was death, were said to commit a sin unto death, or a sin worthy of death. They were not to pray for the deliverance of such an offender from the penalty of violated law. There were many offences which the law did not punish with death; and the sin not being unto death, the apostles were to labor for the restoration of such offenders and seek to restore them to the paths of virtue and peace, that they might become again useful members of society. Bishop Horne, we think, gives the true meaning of this passage. He says:

"The Talmudical writers have distinguished the *capital punishments* of the Jews into lesser deaths, and such as were more grievous; but there is no warrant in the Scriptures for these distinctions, neither are these writers agreed among themselves what particular punishments are to be referred to these two heads. A capital crime generally was termed *a sin of death*, (Deut. xvii. 6); or, *a sin worthy of death*, (Deut. xxi. 22); which mode of expression is adopted, or rather imitated, by the apostle John, who distinguishes between a sin unto death, and a sin *not* unto death. (1 John v. 16). Criminals, or those who were deemed worthy of capital punishment, were called *sons* or *men of death*, (1 Sam. xx. 32; xxxi. 16; 2 Sam. xix. 28, marg. reading), just as he who had incurred the punishment of scourging was designated a *son of stripes*, (Deut. xxv. 16; 1 Kings xiv. 6). A similar phraseology was adopted by Jesus Christ, when he said to the Jews: Ye shall die in your sins. (John viii. 21, 24). Eleven different sorts of capital punishments are mentioned in the sacred writings."

What is meant then by the sin unto death, was a sin deserving of death under the Jewish law, and for which there was pardon, and the Christians were not to pray for the deliverance of such from the penalty of violated law. But they were to pray for the forgiveness of those who did not commit a sin deserving of death. This we regard as the correct interpretation of this controverted passage, and do not think it had any reference to the immortal world, or the ultimate condition of the human soul.

# HELL FOR THE WICKED.

"The wicked shall be turned into hell, and all the nations that forget God."—PSALMS ix. 17.

THERE is no word in the English language, the meaning of which has been so sadly misapprehended, and consequently been productive of such a vast amount of mental suffering as the word *hell*. It has filled the aged with fear and trembling, the young with terror and alarm, the mourner with suffering, and the dying with dreadful apprehensions of the future. And as a motive to moral effort and Christian endeavor, it occupies a much more prominent place in the pulpit at the present day, than the love of God and the varied exhibitions of his grace and truth. And some professed Christians go so far as to inform us, that, if we should remove the fear of an endless hell, they should have no motive to love God, and would as soon curse Him as bless his name.

In the original scriptures there are four words translated hell; three are found in the New, and one in the Old Testament.

Throughout the Old Testament, the English word hell is translated from the original word *sheol*, which occurs sixty-four times; though it is rendered *grave* twenty-nine times, and three times *pit*. The remaining thirty-two times it is translated *hell*, but it is the same word in the original throughout the Old Testament.

A brief reference to a few passages of scripture, will exhibit the original and primary meaning of *sheol*, rendered hell in the passage that stands at the head of this article. In Genesis xxxvii. 35, we are informed that the venerable patriarch Jacob said that he would go down to *sheol*, mourning for his son. True, the translators have rendered this word *grave* in this passage, but it is the same word that is translated hell in the passage under consideration.

*Sheol*, here, cannot signify a place of endless suffering. It means simply the grave, or state of the dead, to which this pious man of God would go in sorrow, mourning for his son. In Psalms xvi. 10, we read as follows: "For thou wilt not leave my soul in hell; neither wilt thou suffer thine holy One to see corruption." The apostle Peter, in the 2d chapter of Acts, refers to this portion of scripture, and applies it to the resurrection of Christ, he being the one who should not be left in hell.

Job prayed that he might be hid in *sheol* for a season, which shows clearly that it was not understood to be a state of suffering after death. The Psalmist says—"My life draweth nigh unto the grave." Psalms lxxxviii. 3. He did not mean that he drew nigh to endless burnings. Again, in Psalms cxxxix. 8, we read thus: "If I ascend up into heaven, thou art there; if I make my bed in hell, behold, thou art there." Though *sheol*, here, is translated hell, yet all admit that it does not teach endless suffering. These scriptures clearly indicate in what sense the ancient Hebrews originally used the term *sheol.* It had reference primarily to the grave, or rather the state of the dead; though it seems sometimes to have been employed in a figurative sense to denote mental anguish and sorrow, but never to denote eternal punishment.

It had no reference to the condition of man after death, as is admitted by many learned orthodox divines. Dr. George Campbell, a divine of this school, says that "*Sheol* signifies the state of the dead in general, without regard to the goodness or badness of the persons, their happiness or misery."

Dr. Allen, another eminent divine of the same school, says: "The term *shoel* itself, does not seem to mean anything more than the state of the dead, in their dark abode."

And Rev. Dr. Whitby says thus: "*Sheol* throughout the Old Testament, signifies not a place of punishment, for the souls of bad men only, but the grave, or place of death."

Sufficient testimony has been adduced to convince every unprejudiced mind that *sheol*, translated hell in the passage before us, furnishes no support to the common interpretation which consigns millions of the race to hopeless despair.

The context shows that the Psalmist was describing the fearful consequences of sin, and showing that the wicked could not go unpunished, but should receive merited chastisement. The retributive justice of God would follow iniquity, the wicked should be ensnared in their own work, caught in their own net, and be prematurely cut off from the earth. The wicked should be swept away by the overflowing scourge, and be suddenly and unexpectedly hurled down to death. This is evidently the meaning of our text, that the wicked shall be suddenly and unexpectedly turned into hell (*sheol*), or swept down to destruction.

Dr. Adam Clarke says the "original is very emphatic," and thinks it means turned headlong into hell, or *sheol.*

Dr. Noyes, an eminent divine, in his translation of the Psalms, gives the following version: "The wicked shall be driven into *hades*, yea, all the nations that forget God."

Dr. Alexander, Professor in the Theological Seminary at Princeton, presents the fo lowing translation and comments: "The wicked shall turn back, even to hell, to death or to the grave, all nations forgetful of God The enemies of God and of his people shall not only be thwarted and repulsed, but driven to destruction, and that not merely individuals, but nations."

Man cannot sin with impunity; iniquity brings sure and often sudden and swift destruction. We think that the Psalmist stated a general truth, applicable to individuals and nations. The wickedness of the antediluvians was the cause of their being suddenly cut off from the earth. While Noah, the righteous man of God was spared, they were prematurely cut off—suddenly turned into hell—unexpectedly and quickly hurled to destruction, or driven into *sheol.*

The history of sinful Pharaoh and his wicked hosts furnishes another illustration of our text. They oppressed the people of God, broke their own vows and commands of the Lord, and while engaged in their wickedness were suddenly turned into *sheol.* The inhabitants of Ninevah, too, were destroyed for their sinfulness, and turned into hell. And such was the fate of the inhabitants of Sodom and Gomorrah, and Capernaum. They all forsook God — transgressed his commands — and the overflowing scourge came upon them, and they, too, were unexpectedly driven into *hades.* And what, alas! became of Babylon, the Great — the queen of nations, and the glory of the East? Her inhabitants became sinful and corrupt, and were driven to destruction — turned into *sheol.* That great and mighty city became desolate as a wilderness — a dwelling place for dragons — so that even to this day, the wild Arabian dare not pitch his tent there, neither do shepherds make their fold there.

Where, alas! are Tyre and Sidon, and old Jerusalem in all her magnificence and glory? History tells us that they forgot God, became proud and disobedient, filled up the measure of their iniquity, and were swept down to death. No earthly power could save them from swift destruction, so true is it that the wicked shall be turned or driven into *sheol* or hell, and all the nations that forget God.

In the 16th chapter of the Book of Numbers, we have an account of the sudden destruction of "Korah, Dathan and Abiram," and all that appertained to them. We are informed that they went down quickly into the pit, as the earth opened her mouth and swallowed them up. In this passage *sheol* is translated pit. Those referred to went down quickly to death — were suddenly destroyed; and so were the wicked persecutors of Daniel, the righteous prophet of the Lord. We need not seek other biblical illustrations of this passage. Indulgence in sin has a tendency to shorten our days, hence we are exhorted to listen to the voice of instruction and heavenly wisdom, for length of days is in her right hand, and long life will she give unto us.

Under the old dispensation, death was regarded as a punishment for sin — being prematurely cut off from the earth; and hence Moses was commanded to go "up into this mountain Abarim, and die in the mount," because he sinned against God. Deut. xxxii. 49, 50. And when sudden destruction came upon the sinful, and they were swept away in their sins, it was said that they were turned or driven into *sheol;* they were unexpectedly and prematurely hurled down to death.

But, says the objector, if this is a correct view of the subject, and *sheol* means the state of the dead, wherein is there any force in the expression, "The *wicked* shall be turned into *sheol?*" Do not the *righteous* go down to death also? True, all must die; but there is a vast difference between dying on the gallows in shame and disgrace for crime, and dying the calm and peaceful death of the righteous. The wicked should be *turned* into *sheol* — suddenly *hurled* to destruction. Such was the fate of Korah and his company — of Sodom and Gomorrah, and Capernaum. There is a vast difference in going out of a man's house with his blessing upon you, and being quickly *turned* out. The objection is without force, for some were *suddenly* cut off for their iniquity, and in the sense of the Hebrew writer, were *turned* into hell; while the righteous went down to death rejoicing in the God of their salvation.

# OUT OF THE KINGDOM.

"Know ye not that the unrighteous shall not inherit the kingdom of God."—1 Cor. vi. 9.

This language of the great apostle of the Gentiles, was addressed to his brethren at Corinth, who had departed somewhat from the teachings of Christ. He clearly exhibits the impropriety of Christians engaging in any suits at law, under the peculiar circumstances in which they were placed: knowing that the prejudices and passions of their opponents were so strongly excited against them, and the divine truths they professed, that a just verdict could not be obtained.

The tribunals of the country were all arrayed against the religion of the great Teacher, and against those who espoused his cause, and sought to be governed by the principles of his religion. "Now therefore," says Paul, "there is utterly a fault among you, because ye go to law one with another. Why do ye not take wrong? Why do ye not rather suffer yourselves to be defrauded?" That is, it would be better to be defrauded once, than to go to law before unjust men and be defrauded again by an unjust verdict.

The apostle continues his searching address in the following language:

"Now ye do wrong and defraud, and that your brethren—know ye not that the unrighteous shall not inherit the kingdom of God? Be not deceived, neither fornicators, nor idolators, nor adulterers, nor effeminate, nor abusers of themselves with mankind, nor thieves, nor drunkards, nor revilers, nor extortioners shall inherit the kingdom of God."

The design of the apostle was to exhibit the purity of that kingdom to which he referred. It was not to be defiled by any class of sinners. No unclean thing could inherit it. Only those could enter it who were in possession of Christ's spirit of humility and love. Those who worked iniquity were not in that kingdom, for it was a kingdom of righteousness, of purity, peace and joy.

Many have failed to apprehend the meaning of the text, by an erroneous interpretation of the phrase—"Kingdom of God." Many understand this expression to refer exclusively to the immortal state of existence. While this is the more common opinion, it is but just to observe, that learned critics and commentators of different names agree in the opinion, that the phrase, "kingdom of God," refers to the gospel dispensation, or system of grace and truth which came through Jesus Christ, to be enjoyed in the present life, that kingdom which consists not in meat and drink, but in righteousness, peace and joy in the holy spirit.

Dr. Clarke, the Methodist commentator, considers that the expression, "kingdom of God," may have reference to the church of Christ here below. Paul did not intend to teach that the different classes of sinners spoken of, never could be saved, that they could never reach the immortal heavenly kingdom; for he adds immediately, "And such WERE some of YOU, but ye are washed; ye are sanctified; but ye are justified, in the name of the Lord Jesus and by the spirit of our God."

The apostle designed to teach simply, that as long as people remained sinful and unrighteous, they could not inherit a righteous kingdom; but when they turned from their unrighteousness, that they could inherit the kingdom of God, for it was a kingdom of righteousness. Thus saints were made out of sinners, the pure out of the unholy and lost, and being washed and cleansed, through the sanctifying power of truth and the grace of God, they were prepared to enter into the enjoyments of the kingdom of righteousness and peace. The kingdom of God refers to the dispensation of grace and truth, which came through Jesus Christ. In this sense, the phrases, "kingdom of God," and "kingdom of heaven," are used in the New Testament. Jesus came into Galilee, preaching the gospel of the kingdom of God, and saying, the time is fulfilled and the kingdom of God is at hand. Mark i. 14, 15. What one calls the "kingdom of heaven," another calls the "kingdom of God," both referring to the same system of divine grace and truth. The unrighteous cannot inherit this spiritual kingdom, for it is a kingdom of purity and love.

Before we can dwell in this kingdom, we must learn to discipline our natures, to control our passions and prove what is that good, acceptable and perfect will of God, repent of our sins, and forsake the error of our ways, for no unholy thing can enter that kingdom. The first condition of access to its enjoyments is righteousness, purity of heart and life. Man needs no supernatural conversion, no miraculous change of nature, to become a subject of this kingdom. He must open his heart to the spiritualizing influence of divine truth and love, and then he is born of God, and inherits the kingdom.

But while unrighteous, and away from God, truth and holiness, he is out of the kingdom, and while thus lost and sinful, he can have no spiritual, heavenly enjoyment. This kingdom, being of a moral and spiritual nature, righteousness is the requisite qualification to enter it.

No sinner can inherit the kingdom of God, either here or hereafter; but the promise is, that all shall be delivered from sin, the moral creation translated into the glorious liberty of the children of God; every tongue shall confess that Jesus Christ is Lord, to the glory of God, the Father, and so all Israel shall be saved. But the passage under consideration, we conceive, has special application to the spiritual kingdom of the Savior on the earth, the dispensation of grace and truth given to the world through Christ.

Those converted from heathenism to the faith of the gospel, did not fully appreciate at first the nature and requirements of this spiritual kingdom of God. And the apostle found it no easy task to indoctrinate the early converts into the pure faith and holy precepts of the gospel. He taught the necessity of departing from iniquity, after having named the name of Christ, for in no other way could they honor their professions and serve the Master. He taught them distinctly that if unrighteous, they could not be the humble followers of Christ. As long as a man remains unrighteous, he is out of the kingdom, but when he becomes righteous, he enters it. Every righteous man is now in this kingdom, while the moral state of the sinner is such as to preclude him from its enjoyments.

He whose motives are pure, whose intentions are upright before God, who seeks for heavenly wisdom, as for a hidden treasure, and desires to promote the happiness of others, is kind, tender-hearted and benevolent, and is swayed continually by the loving spirit of Jesus, is a righteous man. He is governed by moral principle, deals uprightly, walks in his integrity; and exercised by the loving spirit of Christ, he is born of God, for every one that loveth is born of God, and knoweth God. He walks humbly with God, and inherits on earth Christ's spiritual kingdom of truth and righteousness.

# THE FEW SAVED.

" Lord, are there few that be saved?"—LUKE xiii. 23.

THIS passage of scripture is often brought forward to prove that only a portion of mankind will finally reach the heavenly state. It is said, that if Christ had taught the doctrine of universal salvation to the disciples, it would be absurd to suppose that they would ask him if *few* only were saved. This objection to the doctrine of Universalism is urged with great zeal by the advocates of Partialism, and regarded as quite too formidable for Universalists to grapple with.

In a volume written against Universalism, we find the argument stated in the following language:

"Up to this time it is certain that Jesus had not informed his disciples that all men are to be saved; for it would be an impeachment of their common sense, to suppose that the disciples would have asked the Savior if *few* were to be saved, had he already taught them that all men shall be saved."

Now if there is any argument in this objection against Universalism, it applies with equal force against orthodoxy itself! If Christ *had* taught that only a few would be finally saved — as the objector contends — why did they ask him if *few* only would be redeemed? If he had clearly instructed them on that point, as Partialism affirms, why should they propound such a query? To apply the argument of the objector to orthodoxy, we should say, "Up to this time it is certain that Jesus had not informed his disciple that a part of mankind only would be saved; for it would be an impeachment of their common sense to suppose that the disciples would have asked the Savior if *few* were to be saved, had he already taught them such a sentiment."

The disciples, it is said, would not have sought information upon a subject in which they had been clearly instructed by their Master, and yet it is affirmed, they ask him whether a few only will finally reach heaven, when this had been the main burden of his teachings concerning human destiny! Orthodoxy asserts that Christ taught no other doctrine; that he and his disciples believed that only a few would finally be saved. If so, why should the disciples ask him such a question? "It would be an impeachment of their common sense," to ask him if few were to be saved, had he already distinctly taught them such a sentiment!

The passage has no reference, we conceive, to the immortal state of existence; but has special application to the Savior's kingdom of truth and righteousness which he came to establish in the earth, and to those fearful judgments coming upon those who rejected that kingdom. By the similitude of the "mustard seed," and the "leaven hid in three measures of meal," Jesus set forth the progressive work of his heavenly kingdom, indicating great and glorious results from his system of religion, which should continue to extend till all should feel its divine influence and power.

The preceding verse informs us that Jesus journeyed *toward* Jerusalem, still *teaching* as he passed along. This is supposed to be his last journey to the holy city; and it is natural to suppose that his mind must have been occupied, not only with the greatness of his mission, but he must have considered the fate that awaited him, and the righteous retribution coming upon those who rejected his religion.

The passage we are considering and the

succeeding context, show clearly that Jesus had made some reference to the desolation coming upon the House of Israel, and that ill-fated city toward which he journeyed. The disciples saw the hostility of the people to the Savior and his kingdom, and feeling the need of more light and instruction concerning the success of his mission, and the fate and number of those who should be visited with swift destruction, one says, "Lord, are there few that be saved?" Lord, you tell us of the greatness and extent of your kingdom; behold, how few followers you now have! How can your religion triumph as you teach? You see how small a number accept your doctrine and enter your kingdom. Shall only a few be saved?—saved from blindness, sin and unbelief, and from the judgments coming on those who reject your teachings and kingdom?

The reply of our Lord indicated the nature of the salvation referred to: "Strive to enter in at the strait gate: for many will seek to enter in and shall not be able. As much as to say—"Closely adhere to me; follow my instructions; obey my teachings and confide in my word; my truth shall sweep on, conquering unto conquest; but you should make practical my religion, remain firm to my cause, steadfast in the truth, for only such as endure unto the end shall be saved from the fearful woes coming upon this generation." Comparatively few would enter his kingdom, before severe national judgments should come upon those who rejected him. Then they would seek to enter in, but should not be able. Having filled up the measure of their iniquity, they should suffer righteous retribution for their sins. Those few who gave heed to the instructions of Christ, were saved from sin and error, and the retribution which came upon the disobedient and sinful. The important truth taught, is fidelity to Christ and his heavenly kingdom, under all circumstances in life.

# THE RICH MAN AND LAZARUS.

THAT we may more readily apprehend the meaning of the Savior, and appreciate the important truths which he designed to present in this parable, which we now propose to examine, it is necessary to understand the circumstances under which it was uttered, and consider the preceding context, which has an important bearing upon the parable, and which will essentially aid us in our present investigation.

This parable is found in connection with a series of illustrations that composed one unbroken discourse of our Lord, and was addressed to the same audience, and for a specific purpose. At the commencement of the preceding chapter, we learn the character of the audience addressed. "Then drew near unto him all the publicans and sinners, for to hear him. And the Pharisees and Scribes murmured, saying: This man receiveth sinners, and eateth with them." Luke xv. 1, 2.

Gathered about the Savior were publicans

and sinners, who exhibited a willingness to be instructed by the great Teacher, many of whom embraced his religion; and also were present, haughty, aristocratic Scribes and Pharisees, who were puffed up with a conceit of their own spiritual attainments and religious excellencies. They regarded themselves as the special favorites of God, and sought every opportunity to accuse Jesus and his followers with impiety, and teaching doctrines which were immoral in their tendency and influence. They murmured against the Savior for communing with publicans and sinners, upon whom they looked only with contempt. Jesus, knowing well the character of the people whom he addressed, adapted his instructions to their circumstances and wants—first, by the parable of the lost sheep, which is doubtless familiar to the minds of all our readers.

A good shepherd who had lost a sheep, would make diligent search for it till it was found, and instead of finding fault with a shepherd who should seek the lost sheep, every such effort would receive the hearty commendation of all. There would be rejoicing even, that his efforts had been crowned with success.

Jesus evidently designed by this illustration

to rebuke the Pharisees for murmuring at him in his efforts to seek and save the lost publicans and sinners. The Pharisees contended, and they themselves were not lost, but that the publicans and sinners *were* in this condition, and, consequently, that these were the very individuals whom Jesus came to seek; and hence, instead of murmuring as they did, they should have rejoiced that the lost was sought after and found. The same sentiment is taught in the succeeding parable, with a similar application. When the woman found the lost piece of silver, those around her rejoiced in her successful efforts. So there was joy among the angels of God when the erring child of humanity turned from his waywardness and set his feet towards the heavenly Zion. And if the Scribes and Pharisees were in sympathy with the angelic hosts, then they would rejoice that the lost was found. But they exhibited no joyful emotions that the wanderer returned to the fold of Christ, clearly indicating that they were not animated with the angelic spirit. The successful mission of the Savior is clearly taught in these parables. The lost sheep and lost piece of silver were sought after till they were found. This is as distinctly taught as that they were lost.

By these illustrations, thus skillfully arranged and wisely adapted to the occasion, did Jesus exhibit the preciousness of humanity, lost in sin and error, and then justify his course in seeking the redemption of man though never so debased by sin. All were precious in the Father's sight, and, hence, all were embraced in his divine and holy mission. He came especially to seek and save that which was lost; and the Scribes and Pharisees ought to have rejoiced in the success of his efforts. But instead of this, they murmured against him, because he received sinners and ate with them.

Continuing his discourse, the Savior introduces the parable of the prodigal son, which is full of doctrinal and practical instruction, and which is doubtless, familiar to the reader. Considered in connection with the preceding illustrations, its meaning is so obvious that extended remarks upon it are uncalled for. The publicans and sinners had expressed a willingness to listen to the great Teacher, and accept his instructions—to believe on the Son of God, and enter into life. They expressed a desire to return from their prodigality, to arise and go to their Father's house, where there was bread enough and to spare. They were in a famishing condition, *dead* in trespasses and sin; but returning from their prodigality, they are spoken of as one who was dead, and is alive again—who was lost and is found. The intelligent reader cannot fail to see in the conduct of the "elder son" a vivid portraiture of the proud and self-righteous Pharisee, who is always ready to complain when blessings are meted out to other souls!

Although the fifteenth chapter closes with this parable, yet the subject is continued, as we shall see as we proceed. Jesus unquestionably intended to frame these illustrations so that the people addressed should feel the full force of the truths he designed to convey, and the keenness of the reproof they contained. He thus held up before them a mirror in which they might see themselves. Hence, he introduces the parable of the rich man and his unfaithful steward. The conduct of the Scribes and Pharisees is undoubtedly here referred to. As expounders of the law of Moses, they had been unfaithful and unjust. They labored to serve God and mammon, to administer the law professedly for sacred purposes, but actually to secure their own selfish ends. They perverted the law, misdirected the people in their gifts, wrongfully appropriated to their own use what should have been given into the treasury of the Lord. In this way they made void the law of God through their traditions, and attempted to serve God and mammon. The Scribes and Pharisees professed to be stewards of God, and yet taught the people to transgress God's commandments; and Jesus reproved them for their hypocrisy and deceit. They perceived his purpose, understood the similitude as applicable to themselves, and then they no longer concealed their excited emotions, but showed signs of anger by deriding him. At the fourteenth verse, we read as follows: "And the Pharisees also who were covetous, heard all these things, and they derided him." They were conscious of guilt, and having their conduct exposed, they became deeply enraged. Then Jesus turns to them, and says, pointedly: "Ye are they which justify yourselves before men, but God knoweth your hearts; for that which is highly esteemed among men, is an abomination in the sight of God." The Scribes and Pharisees justified themselves in their wicked perversion of the law, in making it conducive to their own selfish ends; when in fact, they were relieved from all obligations to the law after Christ came, who superceded the law of rites and ceremonies by his own blessed religion.

In still adhering to the law after it was abrogated, by the introduction of the gospel into the world, Jesus showed them, by another parable, that the attachment was illegal, and that they were like a man who should marry a woman who was put away from her husband. And this was the condition of the Pharisees; for they still adhered to the law, were *wedded* to it, after it was put away, by the introduction of the new and better covenant.

With this examination of the preceding context, we are now prepared to appreciate more readily and clearly the parable of the rich man and Lazarus. Through all this discourse of our Lord, the Pharisees had been put upon trial, their conduct examined, the motives of their hearts laid open, and, on being found guilty, full of hypocrisy and deceit, he proceeds to point out the merited retribution for their sins which awaited them.

Jesus speaks of the prosperity of the Scribes and Pharisees by saying, that the rich man was clad in purple and fine linen and fared sumptuously every day. But prosperity had not led them to God; they became proud and haughty, and disobeyed the commands of heaven. They trampled upon the requisitions of the Most High, and were unfaithful stewards of God's law. Their condition was similar to that of Israel, spoken of in the 32d chapter of Deuteronomy. Jeshurun, who here represents Israel, forsook God, who made him, and lightly esteemed the Rock of his salvation. Israel became a froward generation—children in whom there was no faith, and after filling up the measure of their iniquity, the Lord is represented as saying that a fire was kindled in his anger which should burn to the lowest hell, and consume the earth with her increase, and set on fire the foundations of her mountains. This referred simply to the temporal ruin and judgments coming upon the sinful and disobedient. Their severe chastisement is spoken of under the following highly figurative language: "I will heap mischiefs upon them; I will spend arrows upon them. They shall be *burnt with hunger*, and devoured with burning heat, and with bitter destruction," etc.

This account of Israel gives a very vivid and faithful portraiture of the condition of the Scribes and Pharisees, whom the Savior addressed in the series of parables we have considered. They, too, grew proud and haughty, and forsook the God that made them, and lightly esteemed the Rock of their salvation. They were unfaithful to their high trusts, and abandoned the service of God; taught, for doctrines, the commandments of men, and made void the law of God through their traditions. They were soon to be punished for their sins. A fire was about to be kindled that should burn them to the lowest hell. They were to be *burnt with hunger*, and devoured with burning heat. The poor, despised publicans and sinners were represented by the "beggar" in the parable, and the Scribes and Pharisees by the "rich man."

The condition of these two classes of individuals was greatly changed. The publicans and sinners exhibited a willingness to listen to the divine teachings of Jesus — to turn from the error of their ways and enter into the kingdom of God. Matt. xxi. 32; Luke iii. 12. Some of this class believed on Jesus; and being thus exalted, morally raised from their spiritually dead condition, they are represented in the parable as being carried by angels into Abraham's bosom. In becoming *Christians*, they lost their national citizenship, were no longer regarded as Jews or heathen — were no longer Jews or Greeks, Barbarian, nor Sythians, bond nor free, but were all one in Christ. Being Christ's, they were of Abraham's seed, and heirs according to the promise. Gal. iii. 28, 29.

To be in "Abraham's bosom" was a figurative expression, indicating simply, that those referred to were of the faith of Abraham. This language shows conclusively, that the account is not to be understood literally; the absolute impossibility of such a construction of the language, argues conclusively that the language is figurative and parabolic. One man was not in the literal bosom of another! But this we must believe on the supposition that the account is a literal statement of facts and not a parable. But the language is figurative. To be in "Abraham's bosom," was to be in possession of the faith which animated the bosom of Abraham—the faith which found a lodgment in his heart; for Paul teaches, that "They which be of faith, *are* blessed *with* faithful Abraham." Gal. iii. 9.

The rich man also died and was *buried*—a fact not stated of the "beggar"—"and in hell, he lifted up his eyes, being in torment." The word rendered hell here is "*hades*," and corresponds to "*sheol*" of the Old Testament. Dr. George Campbell, a learned Presbyterian divine, tells us, that, in his judgment, it ought NEVER, in scripture, to be rendered *hell*—at least in the sense in which that word is universally understood among Christians. Dr. Campbell, in his sixth Disseration, p. 180, gives us the meaning of *sheol* and defines *hades* in the following language:

"As to the word *hades*, which occurs in eleven places of the New Testament, and is rendered *hell* in all except one, where it is translated *grave*, it is quite common in classical authors, and frequently used by the Seventy in the translation of the Old Testament. In my judgment, it ought never in scripture to be rendered *hell*, at least, in the sense wherein that word is now universally understood by Christians. In the Old Testament, the corresponding word is *sheol*, which signifies the state of the dead in general, without regard to the goodness or badness of the persons, their happiness or misery. In translating that word, the Seventy have almost invariably used *hades*. The state is always represented under those figures which suggest something dreadful, dark, and silent, about which the most prying eye, and listening ear, can acquire no information. The term *hades* is well adapted to express this idea. To this, the word *hell* in its primitive signification perfectly corresponds; for, at first, it denoted only what was sacred or concealed. This word is found with little variation of form, and precisely in the same meaning, in all the Teutonic dialects. * * * *

It is very plain, that neither in the Septuagint version of the Old Testament, nor in the New, does the word *hades* convey the meaning which the present English word *hell*, in the Christian usage, always conveys to our minds."

That is, in his judgment, it ought NEVER to be used to signify endless misery. It never was used in this sense among the ancients, never referred to punishment in the future world as human creeds teach.

The Savior used it in the parable before us in a figurative sense, to set forth the merited retribution of the Pharisees, who were to be brought into a low and degraded condition, just as it is used in the 10th chapter of Luke. "And thou, Capernaum, which art exalted to heaven, shall be brought down to hell. (*hades*)" All that was intended here by the people being exalted to heaven was, that they enjoyed high and exalted privileges, and they were said to be thrust down to hell when those privileges were taken from them, and they were brought into a low and degraded condition. Such was the moral condition and fate of the Pharisees. Once the depositories of God's truth in the enjoyment of exalted privileges, but in their haughtiness, they forsook the God that made them, and lightly esteemed the Rock of their salvation. They rebelled against God; and after they filled up the measure of their iniquity, a most fearful destruction overtook them, which brought them into a low state of degradation and misery. So severe was the retribution, that they are represented as saying: "I am tormented in this flame." This was not a literal flame of fire; it was highly figurative language, employed to set forth the severe punishment about to come upon the Scribes and Pharisees. We have already seen that Moses employed similar phraseology to set forth the fearful punishments to come upon Israel, where it is said that the people should be *burnt with hunger*, and devoured with burning heat.

Jesus knew well that the great city of the Pharisees was soon to be visited with famine, pestilence and war; that the overflowing scourge should be upon it, and that there should be a time of trouble such as had not been from the beginning of the world, nor ever should be again. He knew the terrible desolation soon to come upon the people, that they would be cut off by famine and be *burnt with hunger*, as Israel had previously been. Deut. xxxii. 24: "They shalt be burnt with hunger, and devoured with burning heat, and with bitter destruction: I will also send the teeth of beasts upon them, with the poison of serpents of the dust." Hence they are represented as being tormented in this flame, and, like Capernaum, brought down to *hades*, in a low state of degradation and suffering. Those who received Christ and obeyed his instruction, escaped that flame — were not "burnt with hunger;" while those who gave no heed to his teachings lifted up their eyes in its torments. They rejected the Lord's anointed, and put him to an open shame, and consequently, they suffered merited retribution. They lifted up their eyes in torment, being *burnt with hunger*, and devoured with burning heat.

But Abraham said: "Son, remember that thou in thy life time receivedst thy good things, and likewise Lazarus evil things; but now he is comforted, and thou art tormented."

On the supposition that this passage refers to the immortal world and is a literal account as many believe, then it teaches that the inhabitants of heaven and hell are sufficiently near each other to converse together! The redeemed in heaven, then, see the misery of the damned in hell! And would not such an awful sight render the redeemed unhappy? On earth, imperfect as man is, such a sight would fill him with horror. No man, with a tender and sympathetic nature, could stand by unmoved and see his kindred rolling upon a bed of burning coals. And is there less compassion, less sympathy, less pity in heaven? Does heaven so harden the heart that the mother can be happy there and witness the endless torment of her child, and shout glory to God as she witnesses the misery of her offspring in hell? Would not the mother's heart heave with agonized emotions as she saw her child wrapped in sheets of flame and heard the wails of her offspring? Could it be a heaven of happiness and joy to her? Abraham in heaven, it is said, saw the rich man in hell "lifting up his eyes in torment," and conversed with him.

But this language has no reference to the future world, we apprehend. Once the Pharisees enjoyed exalted privileges and received many "good things," and the publicans and sinners "evil things;" but now their conditions are represented as being changed according to their merits. The parable continues thus: "And besides all this, between us and you there is a great gulf fixed; so that they which would pass from hence to you cannot; neither can they pass to us that would come from thence." If this refers to the future world, as the sacrificial theology affirms, then it shows that there are some in heaven who would go to hell, were they not prevented by the "great gulf;" for the language is: "They that would go from hence to you cannot," plainly implying that they would go if they could do so! And why should not those in heaven seek to rescue their friends in hell? But the subject has no reference to the immortal state of existence. The Savior was speaking of the destruction about to come upon Jerusalem, the great city of the Scribes and Pharisees. When that city was besieged by the Romans, a wide, deep trench was made all around it, to prevent any one passing to and from the city. The wicked Pharisees, who were hemmed in by the enemy, could not pass out; and those without the city, who would grant relief to their friends within, could not then do it; all ingress and egress was cut off — no passing to and from the place, for an impassable gulf was there.

Reference is made to this "great gulf" in the 19th chapter of Luke at the 41st verse, and onward, in the following language:

"And when he (Jesus) was come near, he beheld the city, and wept over it, saying, If thou hadst known, even thou, at least, in this thy day, the things which belong unto thy peace; but now they are hid from thine eyes. For the days shall come upon thee, that thine enemies shall cast a *trench* about thee, and compass thee round, and keep thee in on every side, and shall lay thee even with the ground, and thy children within thee; and they shall not leave in thee one stone upon another; because thou knewest not the time of thy visitation."

This *trench* which kept the people in on every side, was evidently the impassable gulf referred to. No relief could be obtained from friends without the city—not even water to cool their parched tongues. The people were tormented with famine, being *burnt with hunger*, so that Josephus tells us that the inhabitants seemed like ghosts in the streets, and the mother, famishing for food, ate up her own babe. This was the flame in which they lifted up their eyes, being in torment.

The parable continues, representing the rich man as offering a petition to Father Abraham in behalf of his five brethren, that they might not be involved in the same ruin and misery. The brethren referred to were the national brethren of the Scribes and Pharisees, who had not been overwhelmed in the terrible calamities which came upon the inhabitants of Jerusalem, and who had not felt the *burning of hunger*. The prayer certainly was a most benevolent one. The reply was: "They have Moses and the prophets, let them hear them." That is, let them listen to what Moses and the prophets have said concerning the judgments of God on the disobedient and sinful, and take warning. But Moses had said nothing in regard to a place of torment in the future world. This is admitted by eminently learned divines of the orthodox church. We quote the following orthodox divines upon this point, to show that a state of future punishment was not held up as a motive to the people under the Mosaic ecomony:

MILMAN.—"The sanction on which the Hebrew law was founded is extraordinary. The lawgiver (Moses) maintains a profound silence on that fundamental article, if not of political, at least of religious legislation — rewards and punishments in another life. He substituted temporal chastisements and temporal blessings. On the violation of the constitution followed inevitably, blighted harvests, famine, pestilence, defeat, captivity; on its maintenance, abundance, health, fruitfulness, victory, independence. How wonderfully the event verified the prediction of the inspired legislator! how invariably apostacy led to adversity — repentance and reformation to prosperity."

Bishop Warburton.—"In the Jewish Republic, both the rewards and punishments promised by heaven were temporal only. Such as health, long life, peace, plenty, and dominion, etc. Diseases, premature death, war, famine, want, subjections, and captivity, etc. And in no one place of the Mosaic Institutes is there the least mention, or any intelligible hint of the rewards and punishments of another life.

When Solomon restored the integrity of religion, he addressed a long prayer to the God of Israel, consisting of one solemn petition for the continuance of the old covenant, made by the ministry of Moses. He gives us an exact account of all its parts, and explains at large the sanctions of the Jewish Law and Religion. And here, as in the writings of Moses, we find nothing but temporal rewards and punishments."

Paley.—"This (Mosaic) dispensation dealt in temporal rewards and punishments. In the 28th of Deuteronomy you find Moses, with prodigious solemnity, pronounce the blessings and cursings which awaited the children of Israel under the dispensation to which they were called. And you will observe, that these blessings consisted altogether of worldly benefits, and these curses of worldly punishments."

Jahn, whose excellent work is a text-book in the Andover Theological Seminary, says: "We have not authority, therefore, decidedly to say, that any other motives were held out to the ancient Hebrews to pursue the good and avoid the evil, than those which were derived from the rewards and punishments of this life."

If, as these divines contend, no other motives were held out by Moses but the rewards and punishments of this life, he certainly did not teach endless punishment for the sins of this life. But Moses had spoken of temporal calamities, of severe national judgments which were to come upon the disobedient and sinful in this life, and of the people being burnt with hunger, as we have seen. And hence the propriety of directing the people to consult the writings of Moses and the prophets.

They will not credit Moses, but if one should go unto them from the dead they will repent; or, if one were raised from the dead they would believe. But of this even there was no certainty. Jesus had presented the highest evidence to them that he was the Son of God, the Messiah of the prophets, even raised the dead, and they believed not. Let them take warning from Moses whom they profess to receive as authority.

We regard this to be the correct exposition of this portion of the Word of God. To our mind it appears natural, reasonable, and scriptural.

# HOPE OF THE HYPOCRITE.

"And the hypocrite's hope shall perish."—Job viii. 13.

Although these words are often brought forward to prove the doctrine of endless punishment, yet they do not teach so much as a future state of existence. Not the slightest allusion is made to the immortal world in this passage. Look at the context: "Can the rush grow up without mire? can the flag grow without water? Whilst it is yet in his greenness, and not cut down, it withereth before any other herb. So are the paths of all that forget God; and the hypocrite's hope shall perish: whose hope shall be cut off, and whose trust shall be a spider's web. He shall lean upon his house, but it shall not stand: he shall hold it fast, but it shall not endure." All this has reference to this world. It does not say that the hypocrite shall perish, nor be cut off in the future state of existence, only that his hope shall perish. He shall not realize his expectations; he shall be thwarted in his purposes, and defeated in his plans. The meaning is, "The expectation of the wicked shall perish." Prov. x. 28.

This is the first place where the word "hypocrite" occurs in the Bible, and does not fully express the meaning of the original, as Dr. Adam Clarke says. "Hypocrite," he says, "is a very improper translation of the Hebrew." It means, that the hope or expectation of the wicked shall perish, or shall not be realized. Such hope to remain concealed in their wickedness, and to carry out successfully their wicked machinations, and execute their evil plans; but they shall be caught in their own evil ways, and snared in the work of their own hands. Ps. ix. 16. "Your sin shall find you out." Numb. xx. 26. Being thus defeated, the hope of the hypocrite, or wicked man perishes. He is not successful in his wickedness. The wicked man hopes to sin with impunity; but this hope shall perish; his expectation shall be cut off. He shall be punished for his iniquity. He cannot escape merited retribution. God will by no means clear the guilty. He may hope to sin against God with impunity, but his hope will perish. He may hope to succeed continually in wickedness, but in this he will be disappointed. Every wicked man hopes to succeed in his evil plans, to avoid detection and escape punishment; but as God has otherwise ordered, it may properly be said in this respect that his hope, or expectation shall perish. Calamity shall come upon him suddenly. In an unexpected moment he shall be overwhelmed with confusion and sorrow. While apparently in a prosperous condition, he will meet with sudden destruction. As the flag in its greenness soon withereth, so are the paths of all that forget God. Their triumph is short; their prosperity is of brief duration; hence, it was said that their hope shall perish.

"Whose hope shall be cut off, and whose trust shall be a spider's web. He shall lean upon his house, but it shall not stand: he shall hold it fast, but it shall not endure." v. 14. 15. This language was designed to exhibit the sudden and unexpected judgment of God upon the sinful in this life. No reference was made to the immortal world.

# SIN AGAINST THE HOLY GHOST.

"Wherefore I say unto you, all manner of sin and blasphemy shall be forgiven unto men, but the blasphemy against the Holy Ghost shall not be forgiven unto men. And whosoever speaketh a word against the son of man, it shall be forgiven him; but whosoever speaketh against the Holy Ghost, it shall not be forgiven him, neither in this world, neither in the world to come."—MATT. xii. 31, 32.

IT is believed by many that the doctrine of endless punishment is distinctly taught in this portion of Scripture. We therefore ask the candid attention of the reader to the following points:

1. It is maintained by this class of religionists that there are three persons in the Godhead—the Father, the Son, and the Holy Ghost; and these three are one, the true, eternal God, the same in substance, equal in power and glory. If then these three are one, how can a sin be committed against *one* of the persons of the Godhead, and not be committed against the other? The common sentiment is, that a sin committed against the Father, or the Son, is pardonable, while an offence against the Holy Ghost is *never* to be

8ag

forgiven. But how can this be, if the doctrine of the trinity be true? Is not a sin against the Father or the Son, equally a sin against the Holy Ghost; and if a sin against the latter be unpardonable, is not a sin against the former equally so? And do not those, therefore, who teach the doctrine that a sin against the Holy Spirit can never be forgiven whilst all others against the Father or the Son may be pardoned, deny in so doing, the doctrine of the trinity?

2. According to Dr. Adam Clarke, who is good authority among the dominant sects, only a few Jews, who witnessed the miracles of Christ, and ascribed them to the agency of the devil, are guilty of the "unpardonable sin." He contends that it is not committed at the present day. His language is, "Any penitent may find mercy through Christ Jesus; for through him any kind of sin may be forgiven to man, except the sin against the Holy Ghost, which I have proved no man can now commit." Clarke on 1 John v. 16. And again, "No man who believes the divine mission of Jesus Christ, ever can commit this sin."

The text positively asserts that "all manner of sin and blasphemy *shall* be forgiven unto men," except the sin against the "Holy

Ghost," and the same assertion is found in all the parallel passages. If, therefore, it be used to prove the doctrine of endless misery, it can also be employed to substantiate the very reverse; for it as positively asserts that all manner of sin and blasphemy "*shall be forgiven*," as that the sin against the "Holy Ghost" shall not. And if, therefore, there be evidence in this and the parallel passages, to warrant a belief that the "sin against the Holy Ghost" shall *not* be forgiven, there is equal evidence, from the same passages, to believe, that "all manner of sin and blasphemy" beside this "shall be forgiven." We acknowledge that the sin against the Holy Ghost may not have been forgiven either in the world or age, in which it was spoken, nor in that which immediately followed; but we still contend that all Israel will finally be saved according to the promise.

3. The common exposition of the subject cannot be reconciled with the popular view of the phrase, "the world to come," which it is believed, has reference to the future state of being. But how can the advocates of endless misery account for the Savior affirming that the sin against the Holy Ghost should not be forgiven in the future, eternal world? Had he ever taught that any sin

would be forgiven there? They do not believe it, and hence such an affirmation would have been uncalled for, and superfluous. To affirm that a specific sin should not be forgiven "in this world," plainly implies that other sins could be forgiven, and so in relation to "the world to come." Hence, the expression must have reference to a time when, and a place where, sins could be forgiven. As orthodox religionists do not believe that *any* sin can be forgiven in the immortal world, they cannot believe the phrase in question has reference to that world. Then to be consistent, they must interpret the text so that the expression, "this world and the world to come," will refer to a time when, and a place where, sins may be forgiven.

We come now to an affirmative consideration of the text. In order to understand the subject before us, we will inquire,

1. In what did the sin against the Holy Ghost consist? The context plainly shows that it was attributing the miracles of Christ to the prince of devils. Jesus had wrought a good work, had performed a notable miracle, restoring sight to the blind, and speech to the dumb, "insomuch that the blind and dumb both spake and saw." The Pharisees,

perceiving that the people were amazed, and that they evidently began to regard him as a divine being, attributed the wonderful deed to the agency of evil spirits. They did not deny the miracle, but they would not confess that Christ was the Son of God, upon whom the spirit of the Lord, the "Holy Ghost," was poured out without measure. The sin against the "Holy Ghost" consisted in attributing to infernal agency, what was effected by the power and spirit of God. It was willfully resisting the greatest evidence that could be presented, that Jesus was the Messiah of God.

But Christ exposed the sophistry of the Pharisees. They supposed that the kingdom of Satan would remain to all eternity, and therefore could not believe that Satan would employ any means to overthrow himself. He would rather seek the extension of his dominions, than their destruction, and by such reasoning, Christ exposed the falsity of this assertion of the Pharisees.

Mark iii. 30, shows conclusively that the sin against the "Holy Ghost" consisted in ascribing to infernal agency the work of God —"Because they said, he hath an unclean spirit." Dr. A. Clarke says, after quoting this passage, "Here the matter is made clear beyond the smallest doubt — the unpardonable sin, as some term it, is nothing less nor more than ascribing the miracles Christ wrought by the power of God, to the spirit of the devil."

2. What is to be understood by the expression, "shall not be forgiven unto men?" Evidently Jesus did not intend to affirm that it was absolutely impossible for the Pharisees, who committed this sin, to turn from their wickedness, and obtain forgiveness of God. He neither taught that it was impossible for them to repent, nor for God to pardon, for man is called upon to repent of his sins, and is recognized as being capable of complying with the requisition, and the Deity is ever exhibited as a sin pardoning God, as ready always to forgive the returning prodigal.

This expression may be easily understood by reference to the mode of speech common among the ancients. When one of two things was much more difficult to be done than the other, it was common for the Jews to say that one should be, and that the other should not be. And as it would be more difficult to turn the Pharisees from the sin of rejecting Christ than from any other, hence came the expression of Jesus, "should not be forgiven." They had rejected the highest and strongest evidence that could be presented in favor of Christ being the Sent of God, and it was improbable, therefore, that they would ever be convinced.

Grotius, a learned orthodox divine says:

"This form of speech is a common Hebraism; the Jews often said *this shall be, and that shall not be;* not intending, however, to affirm absolutely that the first should be, but merely to show that the last was much more unlikely or difficult than the first. The sense is this: any crime which may be committed, even all calumnies (or blasphemies), which hold the first rank among crimes, may be forgiven more readily than the calumny (or blasphemy), against the spirit of God." See Paige's Selections.

Bishop Newton says, "It is a common figure of speech in the oriental languages, to say of two things, that the one shall be, and the other shall not be, when the meaning is only that the one shall happen sooner or more easily than the other."

Obviously, then, the meaning of the phrase is simply this: that other sins and blasphemies would be more readily forgiven than the sin and blasphemy against the Holy Ghost, because he who should commit this sin would manifest a degree of depravity that would render it more difficult for him to repent of this, than of any other sin.

3. What is meant by the words, "this world and the world to come?" The word here rendered "world," is the same in the original as is elsewhere in the Scriptures translated "ages," and very properly might have been also rendered "age."

Heb. ix. 26: "Now once in the end of the *world*, hath he [Christ] appeared to put away sin [sin-offering], by the sacrifice of himself." Christ appeared eighteen hundred years ago, at the end of the Jewish age, and offered himself once for all, a sacrifice for sin. Here the end of the Jewish economy was called the end of the world.

1 Cor. x. 11: "Now all these things happened unto them for ensamples: and they are written for our admonition, upon whom the *ends of the world* are come." Here, again, the word "world" should have been rendered "age," as every one will perceive.

Dr. Adam Clarke says:

"Neither in this world, etc. Though I follow the common translation, yet I am fully satisfied the meaning of the word is, neither in this dispensation, viz., the Jewish, nor in that which is to come, viz., the Christian."

Dr. Pearce comments on this expression as follows:

"Neither in this world, etc.; rather, neither

in this age, nor in the age to come; i. e., neither in this age, when the law of Moses subsists, nor in that also, when the kingdom of heaven, which is at hand, shall succeed to it. This is a strong way of expressing how difficult a thing it was for such a sinner to obtain pardon.'

Here the following objection may be raised. Admit that "world" means "age," the sin is then not to be forgiven, neither under the Jewish nor the Christian age; hence, it will never be forgiven.

The error of the objection lies in considering the Christian age to embrace the whole of the Messiah's reign, which is both unnecessary and untrue. There were ages under the Jewish dispensation, there are ages under the Christian economy. Calmet informs us that the time preceding the birth of Christ, was divided into six ages; and under the Christian dispensation we know there will be more than one age, as we read of "ages to come," in Eph. ii. 7, when the same word in the plural form is used in the original that is employed in this passage, the one however being rendered *age*, the other *world.* So if the Pharisees did not repent in the succeeding age, they might afterwards. There is no evidence that the Pharisees or any of the Jews were to suffer endless misery; on the contrary they are included in the arms of redemption, for all Israel shall be saved. All are to confess that Jesus Christ is Lord, to the glory of God the Father.

The language "hath never forgiveness, but is in danger of eternal damnation," employed by St. Mark, furnishes no objection to our exposition of the subject. A more correct rendering would be—"hath not forgiveness to the age," [Paige] and would be in danger of "eternal punishment," as Dr. Campbell translates it. The word rendered "eternal," is *aionion* in the original, an adjective derived from the Greek word *aion*, which signifies "age." It is applied to that which is limited in duration, as also to that which is endless in its nature. We can determine nothing in reference to duration, simply by the use of this term. An indefinite period of time is here meant by it, and it would be more correctly rendered "age-lasting." They were in danger of age-lasting punishment.

The word rendered "damnation" is the same in the original as is often translated "judgment," and sometimes "condemnation" and "condemn." Those threatened were to suffer damnation or condemnation. Theirs was the condemnation that light came into this world, and they loved darkness rather than light. Their minds were filled with doubt, and darkness, and unbelief, therefore were they damned: "for he that doubteth is *damned.*"

This we believe to be a correct exposition of the passage which heads this article, as well as an irrefutable explanation of the "sin against the Holy Ghost," and its attendant consequences. Though, like many of our brethren, we were taught by those whom we loved and honored, a vastly different doctrine from this text and others similar to it, from what we now believe, we have long since come to the conclusion that those teachings were incorrect, and have therefore rejected them, and sought another explanation more in harmony with the gospel. This explanation we have given above.

# FEARFUL JUDGMENTS OF GOD.

"It is a fearful thing to fall into the hands of the living God."—HEB. x. 31.

ALL men, strictly speaking, are in the hands of God. He has created all, He upholds and sustains all by the word of his power and He supplies the wants of all by his own bountiful hand. He scatters blessings along our pathway, and the arms of his everlasting love are continually about us. If all now are in his hands, how can it be said to be "a fearful thing to fall into the hands of the living God?"

In different senses, people are said to be in the "hands of God." Speaking after the manner of men, "to fall into the hands of the living God," was to suffer the merited retribution which his hands inflict. As every transgression and disobedience received, from the hands of God, a just recompense of reward, the judgments thus inflicted are said to be "fearful." And as these judgments for disobedience and iniquity come from the hands of the Almighty, it is said to be a fearful thing to fall into the hands of God, or under the divine judgments, or, in other words, to experience the fearful retributions for sin which God inflicts on the transgressor.

Hence, we read that "the hand of the Lord was against them to destroy them." Deut. ii. 15. Of the disobedient Israelites it was said that "the hand of the Lord was against them for evil." Judges ii. 15. That is, the Lord punished them for their iniquity. When the Lord smote the people of Ashdod with disease, or punished them for their sins, it is said the "hand of the Lord was heavy upon them." 1 Sam. v. 6. And again at the 9th verse, we read that "the hand of the Lord was against the city with a very great destruction." The people suffered fearful judgments. When the Israelites gained a signal victory over the Philistines by the help of the Lord, it is said "the hand of the Lord was against the Philistines." 1 Sam. vii. 13. When the children of Israel had suffered an adequate punishment for their iniquity, it was said that "they received of the Lord's hand double for all their sins." Isaiah xl. 2.

The judgments which came upon Jerusalem, upon Sodom and Gomorrah, upon Tyre and Sidon, were all fearful, and all regarded as coming from the hand of God; hence, it was said to be a fearful thing to fall into the hands of the living God. When the people had filled up the measure of their iniquity, it was a fearful thing to suffer for their transgressions. Cain found the retributions of God fearful indeed, when he went out a vagabond in the earth, stung by remorse as the voice of his brother's blood cried from the ground, and in the intensity of his suffering he was constrained to cry out, "My punishment is greater than I can bear!" The antediluvians found the judgments of God fearful, when they were swept away by the waters of the sea. The inhabitants of Sodom and Gomorrah found that it was a "fearful thing" to fall under the divine judgments. When Jerusalem was besieged by the Romans, and the abomination of desolation, spoken of by Daniel the prophet, came upon that ill-fated city, and the people were visited with famine, pestilence and war, then they found by a mournful experience that it was a fearful thing to fall beneath the judgments of the Almighty, or into the hands of the living God.

The context shows that the apostle referred to the divine judgments to come upon Jerusalem. They saw "the day approaching." Verse 25. They saw the fearful judgments of God approaching; the day of judgment to that nation. Dr. Clarke comments on the phrase "that day," thus:

"The time which God would come and pour out his judgments on the Jewish nation."

Those who willfully rejected Christ after they received the knowledge of the truth, and turned back again to Judaism, would be overwhelmed in the divine judgments that should devour the adversaries. Verse. 27. Upon this Dr. Clarke remarks:

"Probably the apostle here refers to the case of the unbelieving Jews in general, as in chapter vi., to the dreadful judgment that was coming upon them, and the burning up of their temple and city with fire."

The apostle refers to those persecuting Jews who had trodden under foot the Son of God, and persecuted his followers. They had filled up the measure of their iniquity, and were to experience merited retribution. "For we know Him that hath said, Vengeance belongeth unto me, I will recompense, saith the Lord." And again: "The Lord shall judge his people. It is a fearful thing to fall into the hands of the living God." This day of vengeance and recompense alluded to the fearful judgments which were to come upon the rebellious house of Israel, when Jerusalem should be destroyed. The day of vengeance was when these severe national judgments and calamities came upon the Jewish people. "For these be the days of vengeance, that all things which are written may be fulfilled." Luke xxi. 22.

God punished man for his iniquity. The judgments that came upon him for sin, came from the hand of God; hence, it was said to be a "fearful thing to fall into the hands of the living God." Yet, God punishes not in revenge. "He will not cast off forever." Lam. iii. 31–33. "He hath concluded them all in unbelief, that He might have mercy upon all." Rom. xi. 32.

# IN DANGER OF HELL FIRE.

"Ye have heard that it was said by them of old time, Thou shalt not kill; and whosoever shall kill, shall be in danger of the judgment; but I say unto you, That whosoever is angry with his brother without a cause, shall be in danger of the judgment: and whosoever shall say to his brother, Raca, shall be in danger of the council: but whosoever shall say, *Thou* fool, shall be in danger of hell-fire."—MATT. v. 21, 22.

THE object of the Savior in uttering these words was to exhibit the superiority of his religiòn over the teachings of Judaism, inasmuch as that took cognizance of the thoughts and motives of the heart, and judged man according to his intentions. Jesus looked beneath the outward forms, at the thoughts and purposes of the soul, and before his judgment-seat man stood condemned if he were actuated by impure motives. In the passage we now consider, Jesus alludes to the awful crime of murder, and to the prohibition given to the Jews in regard to the sacredness of human life. After referring to the legal tribunal before which the guilty should be brought for trial, he points out the difference between his religion and Judaism, and illustrates the principle upon which the laws of his spiritual kingdom are enforced. He came to erect his throne in the human heart, to govern the affections, and hence he judged man according to the *motives* by which he was actuated. Unlike the teachings of Judaism, Jesus taught that it was not absolutely necessary to commit the overt act, to be guilty before God, but if a man wickedly gave way to temptation, and harbored vile passions and purposes, he was guilty before God and amenable to the divine law. He who *hated* his brother was a murderer. Jesus also taught that punishment under his rule was proportioned to criminality, as under the legal dispensation. He refers to three distinct modes of punishment recognized by Jewish regulations. Each one of these exceeded the other in severity. They were, first, strangling or beheading; second, stoning, and third, burning alive.

The lower tribunal or court, referred to in the passage before us, by the term "judgment," was composed of twenty-three judges, or as some learned men think — of seven judges and two scribes. The higher tribunal or "council," was doubtless the Sanhedrim, the highest ecclesiastical and civil tribunal of the Jews; composed of seventy judges, whose prerogative it was to judge the greatest offenders of the law, and could even condem the guilty to death. They were often condemned to *gehenna*-fire, or as it is translated, *hell*-fire. In this place, which bordered on the south of Jerusalem, criminals, it is said, were burnt alive. No allusion is made here to the immortal world, as many have erroneously supposed. Dr. Adam Clarke, the Methodist divine, comments as follows on the phrase "hell-fire":

"Our Lord here alludes to the valley of the son of Hinnom. This place was near Jerusalem; and had been formerly used for these abominable sacrifices, in which the idolatrous Jews had caused their children to pass through the fire to Moloch."

In the old Testament, there are many allusions to this *gehenna* of fire, but there is not a single passage where any reference is made to the immortal world. It is used in a figurative sense to portray temporal calamities and severe national judgments, but never employed to represent endless misery and woe. This phrase occurs twelve times in the New Testament, and is invariably applied to the Jews, the Gentiles never having been warned against it, nor threatened with it. It is, therefore, reasonable to conclude that they were not exposed to it.

Jesus did not intend to say, that under the Christian dispensation, men should be brought before the different tribunals referred to in the text, to be adjudicated, but he designed to show that under the new economy of grace and truth, man was still a subject of retributive justice, but was judged according to the motives of the heart. "But I say unto you, whosoever is angry with his brother without a cause, shall be in danger of the judgment." According to the Christian principle, man is guilty if he *designs* to do wrong. Some learned divines think that the following would be a better rendering of the original: "I say unto you, that every one who is vainly incensed against his brother, shall be obnoxious to the judgment; and whosoever shall say to his brother Raca, [i. e., thou worthless fellow] shall be obnoxious to the Sanhedrim; and whosoever shall say Moreh [i. e., thou wretch] shall be obnoxious to the *gehenna* of fire." Dr. Campbell, a learned orthodox divine, regards this as the correct translation.

Allusion is here made to the different courts among the Jews that administered different kinds of punishment. And the object of Christ was to show that in the administration of his kingdom, punishment was proportioned to the nature of the offence. Christ did not design to teach, that an individual would be tormented eternally for saying "Thou fool;" for both he and the apostle Paul used the expression. Christ said: "O *fools*, and slow of heart." "Thou fool," says Paul, "that which thou sowest cannot be quickened except it die." It is recorded twice in the 23d chapter of Matthew, that Jesus called the Jews "fools," and hence we cannot suppose that he would condemn a man to endless pain for using the term. No allusion is made to the immortal world.

Dr. Campbell, an orthodox divine, remarks as follows on this passage:

"In the common translation of the verse there is a confounding of things present and future — of things human and divine — that badly comports with the wisdom and dignity of the speaker! What affinity exists between judges, a council and hell-fire? Why should an expression of anger, only subject a person to human judges, and another subject him to hell-fire in the usual sense of those words? Now if the terms in the verse conveyed the same meaning to us, which they conveyed to the audience, which the Savior at that time addressed, we should discover a propriety and beauty in them which is not manifest in the common translation of them. The fact is, the allusions in this verse are all to human institutions or customs among the Jews, and the judges, the Sanhedrim and the hell-fire here introduced, are all human punishments!"

This language evidently cannot be understood literally. Jesus did not design to teach that those who were angry without a cause, were really in danger of the "judgment," or liable to be brought before the lower courts of the Jews, that whoever shall call his brother Raca, that is "shallow-brained," or "blockhead," was really in danger of the "council," or the higher court of the Jews, called the Sanhedrim. No one supposes that this is to be understood literally, that an indulgence of these passions really subjected an individual to these Jewish courts. Neither can we rationally suppose that our Lord designed to teach that if an individual called another a "fool," or apostate, or miscreant, or wretch, that he was really in danger of *gehenna-fire*, translated hell-fire.

But Jesus referred to these different offences and grades of punishment among the Jews, to show that under the new dispensation, punishment should be proportioned to the offence, and an adequate retribution would be visited upon the transgressor.

We ask the reader's attention to the opinions of several learned commentators upon this passage. Dr. Adam Clarke says:

"It is very probable that our Lord means no more here than this — if a man charge another with apostacy from the Jewish religion, or rebellion against God, and cannot prove his charge, then he is exposed to that punishment (burning alive) which the other must have suffered, if the charges had been substantiated. There are three offences here which exceed each other in their degrees of guilt. 1. *Anger* against a man, accompanied with some injurious act. 2. *Contempt*, expressed by the opprobrious epithet *raca*, or shallow brains. 3. *Hatred* and *mortal enmity*, expressed by the term *moreh*, or apostate, where such apostacy could not be proved. Now proportioned to these three offenses were three different degrees of punishment, each exceeding the other in severity, as the offenses exceeded each other in their different degrees of guilt. 1. The *judgment*, the council of twenty-three, which could inflict the punishment of strangling. 2. The *Sanhedrim*, or great council, which could inflict the punishment of stoning. 3. The being burnt alive in the valley of the son of Hinnom. This appears to be the meaning of our Lord."—*Com. in loc.*

Rev. Mr. Parkhurst, in his Lexicon, referring to this passage, says:

"The phrase here translated hell-fire (literally *gehenna of fire*) does, I apprehend, in its outward and primary sense, relate to that dreadful doom of being burnt alive in the valley of Hinnom;" he adds (for what reason he does not inform us) "that this, as well as the other degrees of punishment mentioned in the context, must, as Dr. Doddridge has remarked, be ultimately referred to the invisible world."

WYNNE.—"This alludes to the three degrees of punishment among the Jews, viz.: civil punishment inflicted by the judges or elders at the gate; excommunication pronounced by the great ecclesiastical council or *Sanhedrim;* and burning to death, like those who were sacrificed to devils in the valley of Hinnom or Tophet, where the idolatrous Israelites used to offer their children to Moloch."—*Note in loc.*

The meaning of the passage seems to be this: under the old economy all transgression was adequately punished, so under the new dispensation of grace and truth, punishment was proportioned to guilt, and would be inflicted, according to the degree of criminality.

# SCARCELY SAVED.

"For the time *is come* that judgment must begin at the house of God: and if *it* first *begin* at us, what shall the end *be* of them that obey not the gospel of God? And if the righteous scarcely be saved, where shall the ungodly and the sinner appear?—1 PETER iv. 17, 18.

IN examining this passage, let us first attempt to ascertain what is meant by judgment beginning at the house of God? This point, once understood, will aid us in our subsequent investigations. "For the time is come," says Peter, "that judgment must begin at the house of God." Allusion evidently is here made to a "time" and "judgment," in relation to which, the author of these words had been previously instructed. A brief reference to the circumstances under which the text was uttered, will essentially aid us in arriving at the truth originally designed to be set forth. Before the introduction of Christianity into the world, man had long been groping in darkness and unbelief; he had become blinded by sin and prejudice, and wedded to long established opinions.

He had received error for truth, darkness for light, and become extremely superstitious and consérvative, and madly resisted the light and knowledge which Jesus furnished for the instruction and salvation of the world.

When Jesus came to earth to bless poor, erring humanity, in the execution of his divine mission, he called to his aid a number of apostles to be co-workers with him in establishing his kingdom of grace and truth, and in spreading abroad the glorious doctrines of the new dispensation, which were hostile to the teachings of the Jews, and designed to supersede them.

Peter, the author of these words, was one whom the Savior employed to go forth in defence of his truth, and encounter the opposition which a wicked world would bestow upon the disciples of the cross. The Master clearly portrayed the difficulties with which his friends would meet in the execution of their mission. He informed them of the awful woes and terrible calamities which were about to come upon the people with whom they mingled, for their sinfulness. The Savior looked forward to the time when those temporal judgments would come upon the Jewish nation; but before Jerusalem itself was to be laid in ruins, the disciples of Christ would be persecuted, and this should be one of the signs that would precede the overthrow of that ill-fated city, over which the Savior wept. Jesus said to his disciples thus: "Then shall they deliver you up to be *afflicted*, and shall kill you; and ye shall be hated of all nations for my name's sake." Having, then, such a personal interest in the matter, the disciples could not easily have forgotten this sign. "But," says Jesus, "when they persecute you in this city, flee ye to another." See Matt. x. 22, 23; and xxiv. 9, etc.

When the disciples of Christ went forth to preach the gospel of the kingdom of God, they met with the persecution which was foretold; the wrath of a perverse generation was aroused against them; danger and death seemed before them; and Peter then remembers the language of the Master in relation to the signs that should precede the destruction of the Jewish nation. Jesus told them that they would be hated of all men, and be delivered up to be afflicted and killed; and that they must flee from city to city; and when the persecution foretold commenced, Peter exclaims: "The time *is come* that judgment must begin at the house of God," etc. As though Peter had said: "The time predicted by our Master has arrived; persecution has commenced against us; that time which Christ foretold has come." By the "judgment beginning at the house of God," reference is made to the *persecution* which the followers of Christ received.

But, is their any Scripture proof to justify the assertion, that Christians are referred to by the expression, "house of God?" Most certainly, we answer. In Heb. iii. 6, Paul says thus: "But Christ as a Son over his own house: *whose house* are we;" etc. Here, faithful believers are called God's house; and it was with this "house" that judgment was to begin; or, in other words, that persecution was to commence. Again, in the 2d chapter of Ephesians, Paul informed the brethren that they were of the "household of God." That this is the meaning of Peter, seems further evident from the language he employs, before and after the expression we are now considering. He says: "Yet if any man suffer as a Christian, let him not be ashamed," etc. "For the time is come that judgment must begin at the house of God; and if it first begin *at us*," etc. Those who were to suffer as Christians, composed the house of God; and these Peter calls "us." Persecution was to begin at the house of

God. Jesus foretold that Christians would first suffer affliction, before vengeance should be taken on those who obeyed not the gospel of God.

Many Christians did suffer at the hand of wicked persecutors; they were in distress and affliction, consequently the day was nigh at hand when temporal calamities and awful judgments were to come upon the "ungodly and the sinner."

We are prepared to inquire now what is meant by the expression—"If the righteous scarcely be saved?" Christians are referred to by those called "righteous," who are also mentioned by the term "us," with whom persecution was first to begin. Such, by a diligent observation of the signs which Jesus foretold should precede the destruction of *the Jewish state, would be able to make their* escape. The Savior told them to flee to the mountains, and when the time came they barely escaped the hand of the enemy; or, were scarcely saved.

Many learned orthodox divines have given a similar interpretation to this scripture. Dr. Macknight gives the following reading to, and comments on, the passage:

"Indeed the time is come, that the punishment to be inflicted on the Jews as a nation, for their crimes from the first to last, must begin at you Jewish Christians, now become the house of God. And if it begin first at us, who are so dear to God on account of our faith in his Son, what will the end be of those Jews who obey not the gospel of God?

And when God thus punishes the nation, if the righteous Jews, who believe in Christ, with difficulty can be saved, where will the ungodly and sinful part of the nation show themselves saved from the divine vengeance?

That the apostle is not speaking here of the difficulty of the salvation of the righteous, at the day of judgment, will be evident to any one who considers 2 Peter i. 11.... What he speaks of, is the difficulty of the preservation of the Christians, at the time of the destruction of Jerusalem; yet they were preserved; for so Christ promised. Matt. xxiv. 13. But the ungodly and wicked Jews were saved neither in Judea, nor anywhere else."

Dr. Adam Clarke, the Methodist commentator, says thus:

Verse 17. *Judgment must begin at the house of God.* "Our Lord had predicted that, previously to the destruction of Jerusalem, his followers would have to endure various calamities. See Matt. xxiv. 9, 21, 22; Mark xiii. 12, 13; John xvi. 2, etc. Here his true disciples are called *the house* or *family of God.* That the converted Jews suffered much from their own brethren, the *zealots* or *factions*, into which the Jews were at that time divided, needs little proof, and some interpreters think that this was in conformity to the purpose of God. Matt. xxiii. 35. (*That on you may come all the righteous blood shed from the foundation of the world*). 'That the Jewish Christians were to be involved in the general punishment; and that it was proper to begin at *them*, as a part of the devoted Jewish nation, notwithstanding they were now become the house of God; because the justice of God would, thereby, be more illustriously displayed.' See Macknight. But, probably, the word *krima*, which we here translate *judgment*, may mean no more than affliction and distress; for it was a Jewish maxim, that when God was about to pour down some general judgment, He began with afflicting his own people, in order to correct and amend them; that they might be prepared for the overflowing scourge. In *Bava Kama*, fol. 60, 1, we have the same sentiment, and in nearly the same words as in Peter, viz.: 'God never punishes the world but because of the wicked; but He always begins with the righteous first. The destroyer makes no difference between the just and the unjust; only he begins first with the righteous.' See Ezek. ix. 1–7, where God orders the destroyer to slay both old and young in the city; but, said he: '*Begin at my sanctuary*.'

And if it first begin *at us*, Jews who have repented and believe on the Son of God, *what shall be the end of them*, the Jews who continue impenitent, and *obey not the gospel of God?* Here is the plainest reference to the above Jewish maxim; and this, it appears, was founded upon the text which St. Peter immediately quotes.

Verse 18. *And if the righteous scarcely be saved.* If it shall be with *extreme difficulty* that the Christians shall escape from Jerusalem, when the Roman armies shall come against it, with the full commission to destroy it, *where shall the ungodly and sinner appear?* Where shall the proud *Pharisaic boaster* in his own outside holiness, and the *profligate transgressor* of the laws of God, show themselves, as having escaped the divine vengeance? The Christians, though with difficulty, did escape every man; but not one of the Jews escaped, whether found in Jerusalem or elsewhere. * * *

I have, on several occasions, shown that when Cestius Gallus came against Jerusalem, many Christians were shut up in it; when he strangely raised the siege, the Christians immediately departed to Pella, in Cœlosyria, into the dominions of King Agrippa, who was an ally of the Romans; and there they were in safety; and it appears from the ecclesiastical historians that they had but barely time to leave the city before the Romans returned under the command of Titus, and never left the place till they had destroyed the temple, razed the city to the ground, slain upwards of a million of those wretched people, and put an end to their civil polity and ecclesiastical state."

The meaning seems to be, that the Christians had barely time to make their escape, before divine judgments came upon the ungodly Jews; they were with difficulty preserved; or, were scarcely saved from those severe temporal calamities.

Where did the ungodly and wicked Jews appear? What was their condition? Lamentable beyond description. After they had persecuted the Christians, and filled up the measure of their iniquity, the judgments of God came upon them, and they were miserably destroyed as a nation, swept away by the sword of the conqueror. Victorious armies came against them; terror was without, and pestilence within; and their noble city was laid in ruins. The *people* were visited by famine and war, and the ungodly and sinner appeared in distress, being crushed beneath the terrible judgments that were poured out upon them. Having refused to listen to Christ, they lifted the hand of rebellion against God, and were punished as a nation; banished from the presence of the Lord, and the glory of his power. When the severe calamities which Jesus predicted came upon them, then there was great tribulation, such as there had not been since the beginning of the world, and such as should never be again. The struggle was fearful; thousands were slain; blood ran down the streets; and when nothing more could be done in defense of their city, the inhabitants fell to slaughtering one another. The mother even ate her own child, so destitute were the people. And it was in this lamentable condition that the sinner and ungodly Jew appeared. The Christians barely escaped, were scarcely saved; but yet they were preserved, while the wicked were cut off by the judgments that came upon them. They *appeared humiliated—clothed in shame and degradation*—a by-word among the nations of the earth.

We ask the reader's attention to the following, from one who believed in future punishment:

WHITBY.—"For the time is come that judgment must, according to our Lord's prediction—Matt. xxiv. 21, 22; Mark xiii. 13; Luke xxi. 16, 17—begin at the house of God; and if it first begin at us—believing Jews, what will be the end of them that obey not the gospel of God? And if some of the righteous scarcely be saved, i. e., preserved from this burning, [ver. 12,] being saved, yet so as by fire—1 Cor. iii. 15—where shall the ungodly and sinner appear in safety from these dreadful judgments which are coming upon the Jewish nation? Prov. xi. 31."

# LET HIM BE ACCURSED.

"But though we, or an angel from heaven, preach any other gospel unto you, than that which we have preached unto you, let him be accursed."—GAL. i. 8.

To ascertain what gospel Paul preached to the people, we must appeal to his epistles, wherein we find a record of the truths he taught. It is called the "gospel of the *grace of God*." Acts xx. 24. "The glorious gospel of Christ." 2 Cor. iv. 4. "The gospel of your salvation." Eph. i. 13. "The gospel of peace." Eph. vi. 15; and, "The gospel of the blessed God." 2 Tim. i. 8. The significance and appropriateness of this language will be apparent, when we remember that gospel means *good news*, glad tidings of great joy. It was interesting intelligence, good tidings to all people; hence it was called the gospel of the grace of God which bringeth salvation to all men. Even the feet of those who preached the gospel were called beautiful, because they brought "glad tidings of good things." Rom. x. 15.

This gospel brought salvation through

Christ to the world of mankind. Hence, Christ is frequently called the "Savior of the world." "This is indeed the Christ, the SAVIOR OF THE WORLD." John iv. 42. Jesus declared that he came not to "judge the world but to save the world." John xii. 47. "The father sent the son to be the Savior of the world." 1 John iv. 14.

This was the gospel of good tidings that Paul preached, which brought salvation to all men. He preached no other gospel, and he received it not of man, but by the revelation of Jesus Christ.

A brief reference to his epistles will show that it embraced all mankind. He shows that the same "many" that were made sinners, shall be made righteous. Rom. v. 19. And, speaking of the Jews and Gentiles, he declares that "God hath concluded them all in unbelief, that He might have mercy upon all." Rom. xi. 32. "For as in Adam ALL die, even so in Christ, shall ALL be made alive." 1 Cor. xv. 22. He hath purposed in himself, "That in the dispensation of the fullness of times, he might gather together in one all things in Christ, both which are in heaven and which are on earth, even in him." Eph. i. 9. "God will have all men to be saved and come unto the knowledge of the truth." 1 Tim. ii. 4. "We trust in the living God who is the Savior of all men, especially of them that believe." 1 Tim. ii. 10. This was the gospel which was preached to Abraham, saying: "In thee, shall all nations be blessed." Gal. ii. 8.

Paul was made a minister of the truth, and commissioned to preach this gospel of the grace of God, the restitution of all things spoken by the mouth of God's holy prophets. For the proclamation of this truth, he labored and suffered reproach; and yet he was not ashamed of the gospel of Christ, but was bold and earnest in its defence. In the context, he speaks of some who did not remain firm and steadfast in this truth, and he laments that some were so soon removed from the truth, and turned to another gospel which was not after Christ. He saw that some attempted to pervert the gospel of Christ. In the early ages of the Christian church, many spurious gospels were in circulation and Dr. Adam Clarke says that we have the names of more than *seventy* of these *spurious narratives* still on record, and it was because of these numerous and false narratives that Luke wrote his gospel. See Luke i. 1. In some of these narratives, or gospels as they are called, the necessity of circumcision, and subjection to the Mosaic law in connection with the gospel is strongly urged. In the immediate context Paul evidently refers to one or more of these spurious records. He exhorts the brethren to remain steadfast in the truth, and be not troubled by those who would pervert the gospel of Christ. If any one should preach any other gospel, than that he had preached, let him be accursed—let him not be fellowshipped, not be received as a true teacher. Such should be withdrawn from and discountenanced. The word *accursed* here (original *anathema*), seems to be used in the sense of *separated.* If any now preach any other gospel, let him be *accursed* or *separated* from you. Paul applied the same term to himself, and wished himself *accursed* (*anathema*) from Christ. (Rom. ix. 3). The marginal reading in this passage is "separated." This was a strong form of speech on the part of the Apostle to express his intense desire to have the Jews converted to Christianity. He would make any sacrifice to accomplish this, consistent with his religion. In the passage under consideration, Paul designed to guard the brethren against false doctrines and damnable heresies. He proclaimed the gospel in its purity and fullness, declaring that God will have all men to be saved and come to the knowledge of the truth, and that every knee should bow and every tongue confess that Jesus Christ was Lord, to the glory of God, the Father. If any other gospel than this was preached, it was erroneous, and all such false teachers should be rejected and separated from. They should not be fellowshipped. In this sense, the word *accursed* is employed in the passage before us.

Our views are corroborated by the following orthodox commentators:

CLARKE.—"Perhaps this was not designed as an *imprecation*, but as a simple direction; for the word here may be understood as implying, that such a person should have no countenance in this bad work, but let him, as *Theodoret* expresses it, *be separated* from the communion of the church. This, however, would also imply that, unless the person repented, the divine judgments would soon follow."—*Com. in loc.*

CALMET.—"The apostle, in this place, says, If an angel, or if he himself, should so far swerve from the true faith as to preach another gospel, different from that which he had preached, *anathema*, let him be cut off from the communion of the faithful, so that he shall not in any manner be a partaker of the benefits of the church."—*Com. in loc.*

# EVERLASTING DESTRUCTION.

" Seeing it is a righteous thing with God to recompense tribulation to them that trouble you; and to you, who are troubled, rest with us, when the Lord Jesus shall be revealed from heaven with his mighty angels, in flaming fire taking vengeance on them that know not God, and that obey not the gospel of our Lord Jesus Christ: who shall be punished with everlasting destruction from the presence of the Lord, and from the glory of his power."—2 THESS. i. 6–9.

THAT we may correctly apprehend the meaning of this much controverted passage of Scripture, it is necessary that we ascertain first of all, on whom vengeance was to be taken, and everlasting destruction visited, and then we shall be prepared to understand the nature and duration of the punishment threatened. The passage itself imparts the necessary information upon this point. Those who *troubled* the Thessalonian Christians were to be punished with everlasting destruction from the presence of the Lord. And here we are not left in doubt, as the Scriptures are explicit upon this point. The unbelieving, wicked Jews troubled and persecuted the Christians at Thessalonica, as we learn from Acts xvii. 5–8.

"And the Jews which believed not, moved with envy, took unto them certain lewd fellows of the baser sort, and gathered a company, and set all the city on an uproar, and assaulted the house of Jason and sought to bring them out to the people. And they *troubled* the people, and the rulers of the city when they heard these things."

This was at Thessalonica, as the context informs us, and those who troubled the Christians there were the Jews who believed not, and hence it was the unbelieving, persecuting Jews that God was to recompense with tribulation, and punish with everlasting destruction. In further proof upon this point, we refer to 1 Thess. ii. 14, 15. "For ye also have suffered like things of your own countrymen..... Who have killed the Lord Jesus, and their own prophets, and have persecuted us."

Those were to be punished with everlasting destruction who knew not God, and obeyed not the gospel. And of the Jews, the Savior himself declared, "They have not known the Father, nor me." The Jews who madly persecuted Christ and his apostles, *troubled* and persecuted the Thessalonian Christians, and they were to be punished with everlasting destruction from the presence of the Lord and the glory of his power.

This brings us to inquire *when* were the Jews to be thus punished? It was when the Lord Jesus should be revealed from heaven in flaming fire, a figurative expression, denoting severe national calamities and temporal judgments, then about to come upon the wicked, persecuting Jewish people. Christ is spoken of as coming in his kingdom at that time, because his truth would become more permanently established in the earth, and meeting with less opposition and persecution, it would run and have free course in the earth. Proof is furnished upon this point, in the following language:

"For the Son of man shall come in the glory of his Father with his angels, and then he shall reward every man according to his works. Verily I say unto you, there be some standing here which shall not taste of death, till they see the Son of man coming in his kingdom." Matt. xvi. 27, 28.

The coming of the Son of man was intimately connected with the downfall of the Jewish nation. When that old Jewish theocracy was overthrown, and all its oppressive influences uprooted and removed, then Christ came in the glory of his Father, to establish the principles of his religion; hence the expression — "There be some standing here that shall not taste of death, till they see the Son of man coming in his kingdom." The text before us speaks of *flaming fire.* This was highly figurative language, and the sacred penmen frequently employed that figure to set forth the judgments of God upon the wicked, to represent the downfall of nations and cities. In the 22d chapter of Ezekiel, the temporal calamities and judgments to come upon the house of Israel are spoken of under this figure, and it is said the inhabitants of Jerusalem should be blown upon with *fire,* and *melted,* as tin and iron and brass and lead are melted in the furnace. Ezek. xxii. 18–22. This language simply portrayed national ruin. Paul also employed similar phraseology—*flaming fire*—to represent divine judgments then about to come upon the Jewish nation for its sins.

The persecuting Jews had laid up wrath against the day of wrath, had stoned the prophets and crucified the Lord's anointed, and after they had filled up the measure of their iniquity, they were to experience the retributive justice of God. It was a righteous thing with God to recompense tribulation to those who troubled and persecuted the early Christians. The persecutors themselves should be overwhelmed with divine judgments and punished, and the followers of Christ should enjoy comparative freedom and rest.

What is meant here by being punished with everlasting destruction from the *presence of the Lord?* The ancient Hebrews *located* God's presence. They thought it was in some particular *place.* It is said "Cain went out from the presence of the Lord, and dwelt in the land of Nod, on the east of Eden." Gen. iv. 16. "Jonah rose up to flee into Tarshish, from the presence of the Lord, and went down to Joppa." Jonah i. 3. God promised his presence to the children of Israel, in the following language: "My presence shall go with thee, and I will give thee rest." Exodus xxxiii. 14. God was to accompany his people with his presence, and give them prosperity and rest. God's presence was supposed to be with his people in Judea, the holy land, and especially Jerusalem, the holy city, where was built the holy temple, and where the children of Israel enjoyed exalted favors and privileges.

When the Jews were carried into Babylonian captivity, and subject to foreign domination, and where they remained seventy years, they were said to be banished from the presence of the Lord — that is, from the holy land, and their religious privileges; they were then said to be cast away from God's presence; they were driven away from Jerusalem where his presence was supposed to dwell more especially. Hence, we are informed that Zedekiah rebelled against the king of Babylon, until the Lord cast the people *out from his presence.* 2 Kings xxiv. 20. The Jews were driven from their sacred altars, and institutions, and were separated from all those religious associations which had been so dear to them.

But in the good providence of God, they were delivered from captivity and permitted to return again to their sacred land, to rebuild their temple and rear their altars to the Most High. They repented of their sins, and God again vouchsafed his presence unto them.

But in their prosperity they again forgot God, and became a proud, haughty and disobedient people; and again severe national judgments came upon them greater than ever had been, or even should be again. Matt. xxiv. 21. This overwhelming tribulation is called *everlasting destruction* from the presence of the Lord. This sinful people were dispersed among the nations of the earth, they were again driven away from their sacred places, and nationally destroyed; and hence it was said that they were banished from the presence of the Lord, and from the glory of his power.

Their destruction is called everlasting. Not that the punishment was *endless* in duration, for their former destruction which continued only seventy years, was spoken of in a similar way. Paul was addressing those who understood the meaning of such phraseology. They had read of the everlasting hills, the everlasting mountains and the everlasting priesthood of Aaron. The land of Canaan was given to the Jews for an everlasting possession. Gen. xvii. 8. Ex. xl 15. Hab. iii. 6. The statutes of Israel were called *everlasting*. Lev. xvi. 34. Paul employed language very similar to that which the prophet Jeremiah used in describing the overthrow of the Jewish nation.

"Therefore, behold I, even I will utterly forget you, and I will forsake you, and the city that I gave you, and your fathers, and cast you out of my presence; and I will bring an everlasting reproach upon you, and a perpetual shame which shall not be forgotten." Jer. xxiii. 39, 40.

The Jews, as a nation, are now suffering everlasting punishment, and have been for nearly two thousand years; their civil polity has been taken from them, and their former greatness has departed, and banished from Judea and Jerusalem, where God's presence had been vouchsafed to them, they are a reproach and a by-word among the nations of the earth. Their punishment was called *everlasting* or *age-lasting*, but not endless, for all Israel shall be saved. "For if the casting away of them [the Jews] be the reconciling of the world, [the Gentiles], what shall the receiving of them be but life from the dead." Rom. xi. 15. And again, "Blindness in part has happened to Israel, until the fullness of the Gentiles be come; and so all Israel shall be saved." Rom. xi. 25, 26. "For God hath concluded them all in unbelief, that he might have mercy upon all." Rom. xi. 32.

But we may be asked, what had the church at Thessalonica to do with the destruction of the Jewish polity, and the overthrow and dispersion of the Jewish nation? How could such a distant church be sensibly affected, or gain any relief or "rest," as the text has it, by the destruction of the Jews and destroying of their power? They would gain rest by being relieved from Jewish persecution, for in almost every instance the early Christians were persecuted by the Jews who went about stirring up the people and exciting prejudice against the Christian church. It was these wicked, persecuting Jews who troubled the Thessalonian brethren. On every hand, the Jews were engaged in a series of persecutions. They excited the rabble and stirred up mobs against the apostles and the Christian church.

When Paul and Barnabas were on a visit to Antioch to proclaim the gospel of Christ, and the whole city were brought together to listen to the tidings of grace and salvation, the envious Jews spoke against the things they heard, contradicting and blaspheming. Acts xiii. 44, 45. But the apostles proclaimed the truth yet more boldly, and the Gentiles were made glad, and glorified the word of the Lord, which was published throughout all that region.

Then the Jews stirred up the people and raised persecution against these apostles and drove them out of their coasts. Acts xiii. 50. These faithful servants of God then went on a missionary tour to Iconium, and through their instrumentality great multitudes of Jews and Greeks believed. "But the unbelieving Jews stirred up the Gentiles, and made their minds evil affected against the brethren." Acts xiv. 2. Then they visited Lystra, in Lyconia, to preach the gospel, but the wicked Jews from Antioch and Iconium persecuted these apostles, and Paul was so beaten and stoned, that they drew him out of the city supposing that he was dead. Acts xiv. 19. Again, we find Paul and Silas at Thessalonica, preaching with much success, so that many gave heed and believed. But the Jews who believed not, took certain lewd fellows of the baser sort, and set the whole city in an uproar, and actually made an attack upon the house of Jason that they might lay violent hands on these apostles. Acts xvii. 6. They went to Berea, and their preaching excited so much attention that many believed the truth. And when the Jews at Thessalonica heard of this, they came thither also, and stirred up the people. Acts xvii. 13.

Thus we find that the Jews were the chief instigators of the persecution waged against the apostles. Hence, it was perfectly natural for Paul, in addressing the Thessalonian church to refer to the divine judgments which would cripple the power of the Jews and bring rest and comparative freedom from persecution.

# LAUGH AT YOUR CALAMITY.

"I have called and ye refused; I have stretched out my hand, and no man regarded; But ye have set at naught all my counsel, and would none of my reproof: I also will laugh at your calamity: I will mock when your fear cometh."—PROV. i. 24–26.

THIS passage of Scripture has often been brought forward to support the sentiment which teaches that a large portion of the intelligent creation will be endlessly miserable. It is affirmed that the Infinite Ruler of the universe will apply the language of the text to the "finally impenitent" at the day of judgment, a class of individuals nowhere spoken of in the Word of God. It is said that the Almighty will indulge in language something like the following: "I once sought your redemption; I sent prophets and priests, and even my own beloved Son, but you heeded them not. I called and invited you to make your peace with me, but you refused. Now you must suffer eternally; you must make your bed in endless despair. I will no longer seek your happiness, nor be interested in your welfare; but I will REJOICE at your sufferings, and make sport of your misery; I will LAUGH at your calamity, and MOCK when your fear cometh."

Thus our heavenly Father, the God whose nature is love, and who delighteth in mercy, is represented as sporting with the sufferings of his own children, delighted with their wretchedness, mocking their misery, and absolutely laughing at their calamity!

But such a view of the Divine Being is opposed to his nature, which is love, and the revealed attributes of our heavenly Father. He was moved by the benevolence of his own nature to awaken man into existence, and has created all things for his pleasure. Morning and evening testify of his goodness, and innumerable are the blessings which flow from his hand. And being immutable, He never can take pleasure in witnessing the misery of his offspring. He can never laugh at any calamity that may come upon them—never mock their sufferings. A fiend only can do that!

To apprehend rightly and clearly the meaning of the text, we must ascertain the representative being to whom the language is attributed. By looking at the context, we learn that WISDOM, personified, is represented as speaking. She invites the disobedient to walk in the ways of virtue, and warns the sinful and unrighteous of the fearful consequences of transgression, and urges and entreats them to walk in the path of uprightness—in the ways of wisdom—whose ways are ways of pleasantness, and whose paths are paths of peace.

Principles are frequently personified by the sacred penman and represented as speaking. Nature is personified, and the floods represented as clapping their hands, and the fields as rejoicing. Evil thought is personified, and represented as holding a conversation with the Savior. In the 8th chapter of Proverbs, wisdom is personified, and stands forth in the representative character of a female, standing where the ungodly and sinful pass, and exhorting them to be of understanding hearts. So in the context wisdom is personified thus:

"Wisdom crieth without; she uttereth her voice in the streets; She crieth in the chief place of concourse, in the openings of the gates: in the city she uttereth her words, saying, How long, ye simple ones, will ye love simplicity? and the scorners delight in their scorning, and fools hate knowledge? Turn you at my reproof."

Wisdom is still represented as speaking:

"Behold, I will pour out my spirit unto

you, I will make known my words unto you. Because I have called and ye refused; I have stretched out my hand, and no man regarded; But ye have set at naught all my counsel, and would none of my reproof: I also will laugh at your calamity: I will mock when your fear cometh; When your fear cometh as desolation, and your destruction cometh as a whirlwind; when distress and anguish cometh upon you. Then shall they call upon me, but I will not answer; they shall seek me early, but they shall not find me; For that they hated knowledge, and did not choose the fear of the Lord: They would none of my counsel: they despised all my reproof. Therefore shall they eat of the fruit of their own way, and be filled with their own devices. For the turning away of the simple shall slay them, and the prosperity of fools shall destroy them. But whoso hearkeneth unto me shall dwell safely, and shall be quiet from fear of evil."

Wisdom, personified, admonishes man of the way of sin, and portrays the fearful consequences of disobedience. "I, wisdom, have called and ye refused." Who thus refused, or declined to listen to her counsel or instruction? They are denominated here the "simple ones," "fools," "scorners." They who hate knowledge, "who leave the paths of uprightness to walk in the ways of darkness."

What were the consequences of this neglect and sin? Answer: "They shall eat of the fruit of their own way, and be filled with their own devices. For the turning away of the simple shall slay them, and the prosperity of fools shall destroy them." It was the voice of wisdom that called to the sinful to turn from the evil way and walk in the paths of obedience and uprightness. Those who gave no heed to her instructions are called the "simple ones;" they spurned her teachings, cared not for her reproof, but passed on and were snared in the work of their own hands—suffered the fearful consequences of their disobedience and folly. The whole subject refers to the present consequences of wrong doing—the retributive justice of God in this life—without any regard to the immortal world. This is so apparent to the mind of Dr. Adam Clarke, the Methodist commentator, that he wrote as follows:

"Nor can anything here be considered as applying or applicable to the eternal state of the person in question."

To walk in wisdom's ways, was to be upright, moral and just. Wisdom exhorts the sinner to flee from his iniquity, cease to do evil and learnto do well. It entreats the liar to keep his tongue from evil, and his lips from speaking guile. To the intemperate man she utters fearful warnings, and exhorts all to walk in the paths of virtue, saying to the disobedient, "Turn ye at my reproof." But, instead of heeding her voice and obeying her instructions, they rush into sin, and then, when it is too late, they desire to escape the fearful consequences of wrong doing. But now that retribution is merited; all entreaty and effort to escape punishment are vain. Wisdom now could not avert the justice of God, nor save man from an adequate retribution, and, therefore, it appeared like mocking his suffering. When punishment was merited, vain would be the effort of the disobedient to escape it. As wisdom, then, could render no assistance, it would seem as though it laughed at their calamity.

Here is a man who lifts high the hand of rebellion against God and man. He scorns the counsel of the wise and virtuous. Wisdom pleads with him to listen to her voice, and walk in the testimonies of the Most High; but he tramples upon her teaching, and will none of her reproofs. But while rushing into sin, he is arrested in his iniquity and now must suffer an adequate punishment. He seeks to escape, but in vain. He calls upon wisdom to aid him, but as punishment is deserved, shecan render no assistance. She once called, but he refused to listen to her counsel and instruction, and he must now suffer for his folly and sin. Instead of affórding help, it seems as though she laughed at his calamity, leaving him to suffer for his sins.

Now, the punishment is merited; the disobedient call for assistance in vain. She does not answer. Though they seek her now, they shall not find her, for they hated knowledge and did not choose the fear of the Lord. Therefore, shall they eat of the fruit of their own way, and be filled with their own devices, and suffer merited retribution for sin.

Wisdom now calls upon all to refrain from evil and walk uprightly; but if we sin, punishment will be merited, and all effort to escape, apparently, will be laughed at. He who is wise must be wise for himself.

# GOD A CONSUMING FIRE.

"For our God is a consuming fire."—HEB. xii. 29.

THE term *fire* was employed in different senses by the ancient Hebrews, and was a very common figure chosen to represent severe national calamities and judgments, coming upon the sinful and disobedient in this life, but never employed to set forth the retributive justice of God in the immortal world. The people were represented as being *consumed with fire*, and the land as being devoured with fire, and the inhabitants in a *furnace of fire*.

The divine judgments were threatened upon Israel in the following language: "For a FIRE is kindled in mine anger, and shall burn unto the lowest hell, [*sheol*] and shall *consume* the earth, with her increase, and set on fire the foundations of the mountains, etc. They shall be burnt with hunger and devoured with burning heat, and with bitter destruction." Deut. xxxii. 22–24. The judgments of God in the earth, are referred to under the figure of *fire*, and the people being burnt with hunger and devoured with *burning heat.* Dr. Clarke, the Methodist commentator, says:

"All this was fulfilled in a most remarkable manner, in the last destruction of Jerusalem, by the Romans, so that, of the fortifications of that city, not one stone was left on another."

Severe temporal judgments are spoken of under the figure of fire in the following passage: "For there is a *fire* gone out of Heshbon, a flame from the city of Sihon; it hath consumed Ar of Moab, and the lords of the high places of Arnon." Num. xxi. 28. Similar phraseology is employed by David to represent the judgments of God upon the wicked in this life. "A *fire* goeth before him and burneth up his enemies round about." Psalm xcvii. 3.

In this sense God is spoken of as a "consuming fire," because he brought judgments upon the disobedient and sinful. In the prophecy of Isaiah, the destruction of Babylon is spoken of under the same figure: "Behold they shall be as a stubble; the fire shall burn them: they shall not deliver themselves from the power of the flame." Isaiah, xlvii. 14; that is they shall not escape the judgments of God; for verily, "He is a God that judgeth in the earth." Psalms lviii. 11.

In the passage under consideration, Paul uses nearly the same language which Moses had employed when addressing the children of Israel as recorded Deut. iv. 24: "For the Lord thy God is a consuming fire, even a jealous God." Moses exhorts the Israelites to observe God's commandments and walk in his ways, and warns them against idolatry as a sin, God has forbidden and would justly punish, hence he was said to be a consuming fire. The apostle in the context is speaking of things pertaining to the new dispensation, and of Jesus the mediator of the new covenant. If those living under the old economy, did not escape a merited retribution, "much more shall we not escape if we turn away from Him who speaketh from heaven." Verse 25. God is still a consuming fire; He still maintains a moral government and punishes iniquity. He is said to be a consuming fire, because He is the author of those judgments which came upon the disobedient Jews, and destroyed their national existence, or consumed their national life. God punishes iniquity under the new economy as He did under the old dispensation. When the divine judgments came upon the Jewish nation, and the people were visited with famine, war and destruction, God was said to *consume* them, inasmuch as his judgments were upon them. In this sense he was spoken of as *consuming* the sinful because He punished them; thus: "I will send a sword after them till I have *consumed* them." Jer. ix. 16. "God *consumed* the wicked by the sword, by famine and by pestilence." Jer. xiv. 12. When, in the course of Providence, famine, pestilence and war came upon the Jewish nation, and they were overwhelmed in destruction, God was again called a *consuming fire*. This is the meaning of Paul's language, as we understand it. It had reference to the judgments of God in the earth, and not to the endless ruin of a single member of the human family. We present the following concurring testimony from Clarke:

"*Not to the earth only, but also heaven:* probably referring to the approaching destruction of Jerusalem, and the total abolition of the political and ecclesiastical constitution of the Jews, the one being signified by the *earth*, the other by *heaven;* for the Jewish state and worship are frequently thus termed in the prophetic writings.

*For our God is a consuming fire:* the apostle quotes Deut. iv. 24, and by doing so he teaches us this great truth — that sin under the Gospel is as abominable in God's sight, as it was under the law, and that the man who does not labor to serve God with the principle, and in the way already prescribed, will find that fire to consume him which would otherwise have consumed his sins." *Com. in loc.*

WHITBY.—"This shaking of heaven and earth being to be accomplished at the coming of the Messiah, or the *desire of all nations*, cannot signify the removal and subversion of the material heavens and earth, they being not thus shaken at Christs coming, but this is a metaphor frequently used in the prophets, to signify the subversion of a state and kingdom, and of the government which obtains amongst them. Isa. xiii. 13, xxiv. 19–20, Joel ii. 10, Judges v. 4, Psalm lxxvii. 18.

*Consuming fire:* to consume thine enemies if thou obey him, and to *briny them down before thy face*, (Deut. ix. 3), but to consume thee, if thou forget the covenant thou hast made with him. Deut. iv. 24. This has relation to the Shekinah, or glorious presence of God, *the sight of which was like devouring fire*, (Exod. xxiv. 17), and from which went out *fire to consume* Nadab and Abihu, (Lev. x. 2), and those two hundred and fifty persons who burned incense, (Num. xvi. 35), and of whom the psalmist speaketh in these words: *A fire burned in their congregation, the flame burnt up the wicked.* Psalm cvi. 18." *Annot. in loc.*

# SOUL AND BODY IN HELL.

"And fear not them which kill the body, but are not able to kill the soul: but rather fear Him which is able to destroy both soul and body in hell."—Matt. x. 28.

This language was addressed to the disciples by their Lord and Master, under peculiarly trying circumstances. One prominent object of the Savior, as we learn by the context, was to inspire confidence in God, the universal Father. Jesus labored to impress upon the disciples the necessity of fearing God more than all others — more than all earthly tribunals, magistrates, governors, councils, and malignant persecutors. God is worthy the confidence and regard of all, exhibiting a father's interest in all — even the sparrows fall not to the ground without the notice of our heavenly Father. He cares for the bird and the flower, clothes the field with grass, and paints the lily of the valley — and shall He not care for his own intelligent offspring, created in the divine image? Why, the very hairs of your head are all numbered:

"Fear ye not, therefore, ye are more value than many sparrows." As though the Savior had said to the disciples, If God, whom you are called upon to fear, cares thus for the irrational creation, you need not distrust Him, He will care for his own children endowed with intellectual, moral and religious powers which render them akin to the Infinite Mind. Jesus did not design to fill the soul with terror and alarm, and the fear which has torment, but to lead man into a calm and sublime trust in God.

When Jesus commissioned his disciples to preach the gospel of the kingdom, he sent them out as sheep in the midst of wolves, to wrestle with principalities and powers, and spiritual wickedness in high places. They were surrounded by those who thirsted for their blood; hence the admonition of their Master: "Be ye therefore as wise as serpents, but harmless as doves." Preach the gospel of the kingdom faithfully, but excite no unnecessary opposition. Beware of men, for they will deliver you up to councils and bring you before governors and kings, still have faith in God who will assist you in every emergency. Fear them not, proclaim the truth openly, conceal nothing to escape persecution; fear not them who kill the body but are not able to kill the soul. Fear not those persecutors, be not intimidated and deny the truth, powerful as they are; there is a power superior to all councils and magistrates. Jesus endeavored to make his disciples feel that their strength was in God, and if they should become timid and frightened at the power which could take their lives; surely, then, on this ground they should fear God, for He had ability to do this, which was the utmost that their persecutors could do — and infinitely more. He had the power to strike the soul (*psuche*) out of existence as well as the body. God had the ability so to destroy man that he should not exist at all. The Being who can give existence can withhold that existence, and annihilate man in the twinkling of an eye. He has ability to do this.

The word *psuche* is rendered "life," "soul," "souls," "mind," "heart," and "minds." We need not pause here to refer to the numerous passages where it is rendered *life*. All concede that it is frequently used in the sense of animal life, or existence on earth. It will not do, however, to bend every text to this definition, as all can see by an examination of the passages where it occurs. It is rendered "minds" in Acts

xiv. 2. "And made their minds (*psuche*) evil affected against the brethren." This certainly cannot mean merely the animal life. Again, "with one mind (*psuche*) striving together for the faith of the gospel." Phil. i. 27. This cannot well be understood to mean merely earthly existence, or animal life! Again, Paul speaks of "doing the will of God from the heart." (*psuche*). Eph. vi. 6. Once more, "Lest ye be wearied and faint in your minds." (*psuche*). Heb. xii. 3. As this word has a variety of renderings, so has it a variety of significations. Conceding that it frequently means life, we now remark that it appears to be used in a much more comprehensive sense, and to embrace ALL of man, not merely the animal, but the moral and spiritual part of his being — the entire nature. It embraces what constitutes our personality or individualism — the whole being called MAN. It is sometimes used in the sense of *persons*, and sometimes it appears to have special reference to the moral and spiritual nature — as in Matt. xi. 29, "Learn of me.... and ye shall find rest unto your souls." (*psuche*). Christ said, "My soul (*psuche*) is exceeding sorrowful, even unto death." Matt. xxvi. 38. It was his mind or spiritual nature that was exceeding sorrowful. And so when Mary rejoicingly said, "My soul (*psuche*) doth magnify the Lord," Luke i. 46; she meant that her whole moral and spiritual nature magnified the Lord — that her affectional nature was moved and went out toward God. So we read that "Fear came upon every soul" (*psuche*), that is, upon every person. Again, "Every soul, (*psuche*) which will not hear that prophet." Acts iii. 23. This means every individual. So we read of "Three-score and fifteen souls," that is *persons*. "Let every soul (*psuche*) be subject unto the higher powers." Rom. xiii. 1. This means, *let* every person, etc. Again we read of the "Hope we have as an anchor of the soul." (*psuche*). Heb. vi. 19. The *soul* in this passage evidently refers to the moral and spiritual nature of man, for the Christian hope could alone satisfy its wants and be its anchor.

These references are sufficiently numerous to indicate the sense in which this word, *psuche*, rendered soul in the passage which stands at the head of this article, was used by the sacred penman.

Christ exhorted the disciples *not* to fear them who could kill the body, that is, destroy the animal life; their persecutors could do that; but they were not able to kill the soul, hence, soul here must mean something besides the life, or animal existence, for they certainly would take that away in killing the body, but, they were *not* able to kill the soul. If soul here means mere animal life, then the persecutors could destroy it, or kill it, but the passage asserts that they were not able to kill the soul, though they could kill the body!

Soul here must embrace the whole man, the entire moral and spiritual nature, the same as when Christ said, "Ye shall find rest to your souls," and "My soul is exceeding sorrowful." The enemies of the truth could kill the body, but could not destroy the spiritual part of man, but the infinite God could destroy soul and body in *gehenna.* He could annihilate man. He who could awaken man into existence, could sweep him away forever. The truth inculcated was, that God was the proper object of fear and trust. He was greater than all, and should be feared above all and loved before all. Under all circumstance, and in every emergency, the disciples were to trust in God. This was the great truth taught, and not that God *would* destroy soul and body in hell. (*gehenna*).

To destroy both soul and body in hell, or

*gehenna*, was a proverbial expression to denote complete destruction — utter extinction. The persecutors of the disciples might cast them into *gehenna-fire*, or burn them in the valley of Hinnom. This was the utmost they could do; or, as Luke expresses it, "After that have no more that they can do." But God could do more, for he could cause the utter extinction of man — annihilate him even. But it does not follow that God would so exercise his power. On another occasion Jesus exhibited the power of God by saying that He is "*able* of these stones to raise up children unto Abraham." Matt. iii. 9. Not that God would actually exercise his power in that way, and raise up children unto Abraham from the stones of the streets, but that He was able to do this. So He was able to destroy man utterly — annihilate him. As God was greater than all, therefore He was to be feared more than all. Jesus sought to inspire confidence in God, and to have his disciples true to his cause amidst the severest trials and persecutions of life.

# THE WICKED DRIVEN AWAY.

"The wicked is driven away in his wickedness; but the righteous hath hope in his death."—PROV. xiv. 32.

THIS passage has been frequently brought forward to support the doctrine that the wicked will be driven by our heavenly Father, into the flames of hell, and tormented eternally; a doctrine which is dishonorable to God, and opposed to the teachings of his word. Certainly the passage does not assert that the wicked are to be driven into endless punishment; besides, it is conceded by the most eminent orthodox divines, that the ancient Hebrews were not threatened with the doctrine of endless punishment. Dr. Jahn, in his "Biblical Archæology," a standard work with orthodox divines, page 398, says:

"We have no authority, therefore, decidedly to say, that any other motives were held out to the ancient Hebrews to pursue the good and to avoid the evil, than those which were derived from *the rewards and punishments of this life.*"

If the ancient Hebrews, as is here admitted, had no motive to pursue the good and avoid the evil, but the rewards and punishments of *this life*, then the passage under consideration has no reference to the immortal world. When Solomen says that the wicked is *driven* away in his wickedness, we understand him to mean what David meant, when he said, "the wicked shall be *turned* into hell." [*sheol*]. They were suddenly *driven* to destruction, quickly *turned* into *sheol.* Solomon means that the wicked shall be suddenly destroyed—their career unexpectedly ended — while engaged in their iniquity, they would be cut off; but the righteous had hope in their death—that is, the death of the wicked gave hope to the righteous. The sudden destruction of Pharaoh and his hosts in the Red Sea, was the hope of the children of Israel. Then the wicked were driven away in their wickedness, but the righteous had hope in their death. Haman, who had purposed the slaughter of the Jews, was suddenly arrested in his evil course, driven away in his wickedness, and those whose destruction he had planned had hope in his death, inasmuch as they escaped persecution and death themselves. God's people were then delivered from the hand of the oppressor, and they hoped to be free from persecution.

When Jerusalem was destroyed, and its streets were red with the blood of the slain, and the power of that proud and haughty people was taken from them by the Romans, then again were the wicked driven away in their wickedness; but their death gave hope to the righteous. The disciples of Christ were no longer persecuted by them, as before, and the word of God grew mightily and prevailed. Our revolutionary fathers had hope only in the death of those who sought to enslave them and deprive them of their inalienable rights; and after they drove their wicked oppressors away in their wickedness, they had hope for American freedom. Whenever the wicked persecute the righteous, and threaten their liberty and lives, if they are thwarted in their purposes and meet with overwhelming destruction, their death brings hope to the righteous, for they then know that they are free from the persecution, to which they were exposed when encompassed by their enemies. Whenever the wicked are thwarted in their designs, we have hope for the immediate triumph of the cause they oppose. And often the only hope of the righteous is the death of the wicked. Old tyrants never take their heel from the necks of the oppressed until driven from their corrupt thrones. The righteous have hope when they are driven away in their wickedness.

When the despots of the earth are cut off in their mad career, then persecution ceases, the oppressed go free, and the cause of humanity triumphs.

In this sense, the death of the wicked is an occasion of hope to the righteous. This we think was the meaning of Solomon when he penned the language we have considered. Though the subject had no reference to the immortal world, yet, through the teachings of the gospel, we are led to hope for the ultimate redemption of all souls, and that finally every tongue shall confess that Jesus Christ is Lord to the glory of God the Father. Bishop Warburton, speaking of this passage, says:

"The righteous hath hope that he shall be delivered from most imminent dangers." So the Psalmist says: "Upon them that hope in his mercy, to deliver their souls from death and to keep them alive in famine." And again, "Thou hast delivered my soul from death; wilt not Thou deliver my feet from falling, that I may walk before God in the light of the living."—*Divine Legation, Book VI., Lec. 3.*

# IMPOSSIBLE TO RENEW THEM.

"For *it is* impossible for those who were once enlightened, and have tasted of the heavenly gift, and were made partakers of the Holy Ghost, And have tasted the good word of God, and the powers of the world to come, If they shall fall away, to renew them again unto repentance; seeing they crucify to themselves the Son of God afresh, and put *him* to an open shame."—HEB. vi. 4–6.

THE chief difficulty to a correct understanding of this language of the apostle, has arisen from the supposition that he intended to teach that it was absolutely impossible to renew those to repentance, who had once tasted of the joys of Christian salvation, and afterwards turned away from the truth. Divine truth and grace were given especially to enlighten the mind and purify the heart, and man, therefore, cannot become so lost in sin and blinded by error, that God's grace cannot enlighten and save him—that it is absolutely impossible for God to restore his moral perceptions, quicken his understanding and reclaim him from his iniquity. The disciples of Christ, even after they had been enlightened and tasted the heavenly gift, fell away from the truth, and yet they were renewed again to repentance. One denied the Savior, and another betrayed him, and all forsook him and fled, they became faithless and unbelieving, and Jesus upbraided them for their unbelief and hardness of heart. But they were again renewed unto repentance and received their Lord and Master again. Judas repented that he had betrayed innocent blood, and Peter that he had denied his Lord.

God giveth repentance to Israel, and forgiveness of sins, and through the agency of his grace, He can reclaim the most hardened and rebellious. We should not understand Paul to teach that it is *impossible* for God to renew man to repentance, and restore those who have fallen away, for there is nothing impossible with Him. None can pass beyond the reach of his infinite grace.

The apostle designed to teach no more than this—that when persons had been once enlightened by the truth, and tasted the good word of God and the powers of the world to come, and had been convinced of nature and divinity of Christ's mission; if such should "fall away," it would be *more difficult* to reclaim or "renew" them again unto repentance, than to convince them first o the excellency of the gospel — not because the testimony in favor of the truth would be insufficient, but because the mind would be full of prejudice, and such would be in a position unfavorable to examine testimony and weigh evidence impartially — having apostatized, they would have no disposition to receive the word and be renewed again to repentance. If it is absolutely *impossible* for an individual to repent, of course, he is relieved from all moral obligation to make any effort in that direction.

This scripture was originally addressed to those who were in danger of apostatizing from the faith they had embraced. They were in danger of "falling away" from the truth, and returning to the beggarly elements of Judaism. This language was addressed to believing Jews in and about Jerusalem, a very few years previous to the destruction of that city by the Romans. Paul exhorted the brethren to be faithful unto the end, to remain steadfast and immovable. He had witnessed the apostacy of some and the coldness and indifference of others; hence, he exhorted the Hebrew brethren, "Not to forsake the assembling of themselves together," after the manner of some, but to be true disciples of the cross, and never swerve from the truth, so much the more as they saw the day approaching. The brethren were exhorted to fidelity in the good work, inasmuch as it would be very difficult to renew again to repentance such as should fall away. It would be nearly impossible for any human being to present convincing testimony to the the minds of such, and bring them back again to the faith of the gospel. It is more difficult to create renewed interest in the heart of a man, after he has abandoned the truth and lost all interest in religious themes and institutions, and "fallen away" from his first love, than to bring him to the knowledge of the truth at first. When a man falls back into any evil habit which he has once forsaken, we all know that it is more difficult to reclaim him the second time and bring him to repentance. This is what Paul teaches in relation to Christianity. When a man has embraced the gospel, and tasted the joys of the world to come, if he should abandon the truth, apostatize from the faith and go back to Judaism—called the beggarly elements of the world—it would be far more difficult to renew him again to repentance, than to convince him of the truth at first.

The passage before us shows how hard it is to regain a good position when once abandoned; how difficult it is to be brought back to the way of truth and right, when once forsaken, not that it is absolutely impossible for God to change the mind and convert the soul, but that it is extremely difficult for man to present any argument which will turn such from their errors. In addition to what we have said, we ask the reader's attention to the following, from eminent orthodox divines, in corroboration of what we have said. Dr. Macknight comments as follows:

"The apostle does not mean that it is impossible for God to renew a second time by repentance, an apostate; but that it is impossible for the ministers of Christ to convert a second time to the faith of the gospel, one who, after being made acquainted with all the proofs by which God has thought fit to establish Christ's mission, shall allow himself to think him an imposter, and renounce his gospel. The apostle, knowing this, was anxious to give the Hebrews just views of the ancient oracles, in the hope that it would prevent them from apostatizing."

Rosenmuller, a celebrated German theologian, says:

"*Adunaton*, in this place, does not mean absolutely *impossible*, but rather a thing so difficult, that it may be nearly impossible; thus we are accustomed to say of very many things, in common conversation."

# THE JUDGMENT DAY.

"It shall be more tolerable for the land of Sodom and Gomorrah, in the day of judgment, than for that city."—MATT. x. 15.

"It shall be more tolerable for Tyre and Sidon at the day of judgment, than for you."—MATT. xi. 22.

MANY erroneous ideas obtain in the Christian world in regard to the "day of judgment" referred to in this passage. It has been long taught that there will be a day of general judgment in the future, immortal world, when all men will receive their final sentence from the Almighty, and some will be acquitted and pronounced worthy of everlasting bliss, and others will be condemned to regions of despair, where they will suffer as long as the pillars of God's throne shall stand. But the Scriptures, we are happy to say, furnish no evidence in support of such a sentiment. The Bible speaks of a judgment, but not in eternity. We nowhere read in the Scriptures that God will judge man in the resurrection world, but that He judges him in the earth. We never read of mankind *going* into the future world to be judged; but that God and Christ *come* to this world to judge man. Ps. xcvi. 13. "Verily He is a God that *judgeth in the earth.*" Ps. lviii. 11. Again: "He shall not fail nor be discouraged, till He have set *judgment in the earth.*" Isa. xlii. 4. "For the Father judgeth no man, but hath committed all judgment unto the Son." John v. 22. Hence, Jesus said: "For *judgment* I am come into this world." John ix. 39. Jesus came to establish his kingdom of truth and righteousness in the earth; and more than eighteen hundred years ago it was said: "Now is *the judgment of this world.*" John xii. 31. "Fear God, and give glory to Him, for *the hour of his judgment is come.*"

In all these passages, not the least hint is given that God judges man in eternity. In what sense then shall we understand the language, "It shall be more tolerable for Tyre and Sidon, at the day of judgment than for thee." It means simply that the divine judgments which came upon Tyre and Sidon, Sodom and Gomorrah, severe as they were, were more tolerable, or, less severe, than the judgments which came upon the Jewish people, after they had filled up the measure of their iniquity. In this way, Jesus sought to impress upon the people a sense of their guilt, and indicated the severity of the divine judgments about to come upon the rebellious house of Israel. The judgments which came upon Tyre and Sidon, Sodom and Gomorrah, were more tolerable than those that came upon Jerusalem. Greater calamity came upon the Jewish people for their sins, than came upon Tyre and Sidon. Hence, we read as follows, in Lam. iv. 6: "For the punishment of the iniquity of the daughter of my people is *greater* than the punishment of the sin of Sodom, that was overthrown in a moment and no hand stayed on her." Here a comparison is instituted between the punishment of Sodom and Jerusalem; the punishment of the Jewish people was greater; the calamity which came upon Tyre and Sidon was more tolerable, or less severe.

This has regard to national judgments and temporal ruin. It cannot refer to endless punishment, as human creeds teach, for no punishment could be greater than that. If Tyre and Sidon, Sodom and Gomorrah suffered endlessly, then the punishment of the daughter of my people could not be *greater*. But no reference was made to endless punishment. When Jerusalem was destroyed, there was a time of trouble such as had never been before nor ever should be again,

Matt. xxiv. 21. All other judgments, compared with this, were less severe, or more tolerable.

We are able to confirm and sustain this interpretation by learned orthodox commentators.

HAMMOND.—"I assure you, the punishment or destruction that will light upon that city will be such, that the destruction of Sodom shall appear to have been more tolerable than that. See note on Matt. iii. 2."

Again he says:

"Shall be more tolerable for Sodom in that day: i. e., not in the day of judgment to come, for that belongs to each particular person, not whole cities together, but in that day of the kingdom of God, than for that refractory city. God's dealing with Sodom in the day of their destruction with fire and brimstone shall be acknowledged to have been more supportable, than his dealing with such contumacious, impenitent cities of Judea. Com on Matt. iii. 2."

PIERCE.—"That is, in the day of the destruction of the Jewish state, called the *coming of the Son of man.* Verse 23. The sense of this verse seems to be this: That, which formerly befell Sodom and Gomorrah, was more tolerable, than what shall befall this city. That *the day of judgment* here mentioned is to be thus understood, appears from what is said concerning Capernaum in chapter xi. 23, compared with verses 22–24, of the same chapter."

WAKEFIELD.—"*In a day of vengeance, punishment*, or *trial*. This is undoubtedly the genuine sense of the phrase, which has not the least reference to the day of general judgment. All that our Savior intends to say is, that, when the temporal calamities of that place come upon it, they will be more severe than even those of Sodom and Gomorrah. See this phrase employed in precisely the same meaning by the LXX., in Prov. vi. 34, where, instead of *kriseos*, *Aquila and Theodation* have *ekdikeseos;* Isa. xxxiv. 8, and my Commentary on this place. Our Savior, I apprehend, had Jerusalem principally in view in this declaration."

CLARKE.—"*In the day of judgment*, or *punishment;* perhaps not meaning the day of *general judgment*, nor the day of the destruction of the Jewish state by the Romans; but a *day* in which God should send punishment on that particular city, or on that person, for their crimes; so that the day of judgment of Sodom and Gomorrah, was the time in which the Lord destroyed them by fire and brimstone, from the Lord out of heaven."

# ETERNAL JUDGMENT.

"Therefore leaving the principles of the doctrine of Christ, let us go on unto perfection; not laying again the foundation of repentance from dead works, and of faith toward God, of the doctrine of baptisms, and of laying on of hands, and of resurrection of the dead, and of eternal judgment."—HEB. vi. 1, 2.

THIS language, as it stands in our English version of the Scriptures, does not fully and clearly express the apostle's meaning. As the words now stand, the passage teaches that believers were to *abandon* or *leave* the principles of the doctrine of Christ, to go on unto perfection. It is absurd to suppose that Paul designed to affirm that the Hebrew Christians ought to forsake or leave the fundamental principles of Christianity and doctrines of Christ, in order to go on unto perfection, for in the immediate context the apostle speaks of their deficiency in those principles, and need of instruction in the oracles of truth. He says, "For when for the time, ye ought to be teachers, ye have need that one teach you again, which be the first principles of the oracles of God; and are become such as have need of milk, and not of strong meat." He would have them rightly instructed in the Word of God. They were not to hold the great principles of the gospel in light esteem. He desired to have them progressive Christians, to make advancement in the virtues and graces of the gospel. Instead of recommending indifference to the doctrines of Christ, he urged them to growth in wisdom and knowledge, and not remain babes in the truth, but to go forward unto perfection; they should not turn back to the old dispensation, nor turn again to the law, which had been a school-master to bring them to Christ. There was a disposition on the part of the Hebrew Christians to return to the ceremonies of the law, and to incorporate some of those ceremonies into their worship, having been strongly wedded to Judaism, it was difficult to draw them away from it. They had been instructed in the first principles of the gospel, but still they were strongly attached to the religion of their fathers, and continued to look back to the law dispensation, instead of pressing forward towards the higher truths of the gospel. Paul was afraid that they would return again to the beggarly elements of Judaism, or ceremonials of the law, and introduce the old form of repentance, the doctrine of baptisms or divers washings, laying on of hands, etc., as recognized by that old Jewish religion to which they were so strongly attached.

Not laying again the foundation of repentance from dead works. Under the old dispensation, a man who came in contact with a dead body, was regarded as unclean seven days. He was to purify himself by the sprinkling of the ashes of a heifer. See Num. xix. 11–19. The apostle denominates this ceremonial of the law, "dead works." Now that the gospel had come, whose author had blotted out the hand writing of ordinances, there was no further need for such ceremony, and it was only *dead works.* He says:

"For if the blood of bulls and of goats, and the ashes of an heifer sprinkling the unclean, sanctifieth to the purifying of the flesh, how much more shall the blood of Christ, who, through the eternal spirit offered himself without spot to God, purge your conscience from dead works to serve the living God." Heb. ix. 13, 14.

All such forms and ceremonies under the gospel dispensation were useless, hence, he calls them *dead works.* If the Jew could be purified by the ashes of a heifer, how much greater the purification by the offering of Christ. Now, all were to look to Christ, and under this new economy, there was no necessity of returning to the law or laying again the foundation of repentance from dead works as formerly. These things had passed, and the Jew, instead of looking back to these, should look to Christ, as the author and finisher of our faith. It was not enough to exercise faith towards God, under the new dispensation, but the believer was to recognize Christ as the true teacher sent from God. The ancient Hebrews had faith in a *coming* Messiah; but Paul instructed the Hebrew Christians, now, that Christ *had* made his appearance, they should not return to the old dispensation, and believe that God *would* send a Savior, and lay again any such foundation of faith in God. They were to receive Christ as the promised Messiah and Savior of the world.

"Doctrine of baptisms."—This form of expression was peculiarly Jewish, and shows that reference was made to the ceremonies of the law. Under the gospel era, there was "one Lord, one faith, *one* baptism," but under the Jewish economy, there were *baptisms*, or washings. Paul calls them "divers baptisms," or "washings." These ordinances were all abrogated by the introduction of Christianity, and constituted no part of the first principles of the doctrines of Christ. Now that Christ had come, the Hebrew Christians should hear him, not adhere to the old doctrine of baptisms, and Jewish washings, and of the "laying on of hands." This refers to the ceremony of the priest, who placed his hands upon the head of the goat, and confessed the sins of the people, and then the goat escaped into the wilderness, or land of forgetfulness. Lev. xvi. 21. In this way the people were ceremonially purified. But now that Christ had come, the people were to be purified by the application of his grace and truth and love to the heart.

"Resurrection of the dead."—We do not understand that any allusion is here made to the immortal resurrection of all mankind; but rather to a resuscitation of animal life, as referred to in chapter xi. 35: "Women received their dead *raised to life again*; and others were tortured, not accepting deliverance; that they might attain a better resurrection." A few instances are mentioned in the Old Testament, where the dead were restored to life again. Elijah raised the son of a widow, and Elisha raised the Shunamite's son. These were looked upon by the Jews as remarkable exhibitions of the divine presence and favor. But even such wonderful events should not turn them away from the higher display of God's favor, as revealed through Jesus Christ, who had demonstrated the doctrine of immortality, and brought life and immortality to light.

"And of eternal judgment," or ancient judgment, or temporal calamities, or judgment of old. It is probable that allusion is here made to the calamities, or judgments which came upon the Egyptians, for oppressing the ancient Hebrews. It was a judgment that was eternal, or forever, as it is called. "For the Egyptians whom ye have seen today, ye shall see them again no more forever." Ex. xiv. 13. Bishop Pierce, an emiment orthodox divine, has the following remarks upon this passage. The common interpretation makes this to refer to the final judgment; and after giving his reasons for rejecting this idea, one of which is, that the final judgment is not called "eternal judgment," he speaks as follows:

"I think, therefore, that the words are to be understood in a very different manner, and *krima* here seems to me to be put for temporal judgments. Thus the word is used: 1 Peter iv. 17, 'the time is come that judgment must begin at the house of God,' where the context will not suffer us to take it in any other sense; compare verses 16, 17, 18. So again, 1 Cor. xi. 29, 'He that eateth and drinketh unworthily, eateth and drinketh judgment to himself, not discerning the Lord's body.' What this judgment was, appears by the next verse: 'For this cause many are weak and sickly among you, and many sleep.' The word *aionios*, which we have rendered *eternal*, I take to respect not the time to come, but the time past, and to signify *ancient*, or past long ago. That the word is thus used without any respect to eternity, we may see Rom. xvi. 25; 2 Tim. i. 9; Titus i. 2. See also these places in the LXX., Ps. lxxvii. 5; Prov. xxii. 28; Jer. xviii. 15; Ez. xxxvi. 2. According to this account of the words, we may consider the Jewish religion as established by the ancient and tremendous judgments, of the execution of which, the books of Moses give an account; such as the deluge, the destruction of Sodom and Gomorrah, and more especially the drowning of Pharaoh and his host in the Red Sea, and perhaps the judgments of God upon the Israelites in the wilderness for their impenitence and unbelief. Of this last he had, indeed, treated before, but not as a foundation of the Jewish religion, but as an example by which Christians might be warned."

# AND WE ARE NOT SAVED.

"The harvest is past, the summer is ended, and we are not saved."—JER. viii. 20.

THIS portion of Scripture has been sadly perverted from its original meaning, and urged in support of the doctrine which teaches the endless ruin of a large portion of mankind. Modern revivalists seize hold upon it to create religious excitements and to frighten people into the church. They tell the people that now the Lord is in the place waiting to have an interview with them, and unless they make his acquaintance immediately, He will pass by, and then it may be everlastingly too late to call upon Him; He will not hear their cry, but will cast them down to perdition, and they will take up the heart-rending lamentation, "The harvest is past, the summer is ended, and we are not saved, but must wail in hell eternally."

This passage has no reference to the salvation of man after death. It is connected with events which have exclusive reference to this world. It has allusion to those temporal calamities which came upon the Jewish people when they were overpowered by the invading hosts of Nebuchadnezzar. He came upon them in an unexpected moment, and cut off all hope of escape, at a season when they could not retreat, and they had made no preparation for flight. While yet they felt secure, they were suddenly overwhelmed, the harvest was past, the enemy was upon them, and they had made no preparation for a siege. Instead of being saved, they were in the hands of their conquerors.

The face of the country in Palestine is much diversified, which gives great variety to the climate; so that when it is excessively warm on the plains, it is extremely cold on the mountains. It is very cold as winter approaches, and it becomes difficult and dangerous to travel the mountainous regions of the country. Hence, when Jesus foretold the national calamities which were to come upon Jerusalem, he told the disciples to pray that their flight be not in the winter, clearly indicating the danger of traveling at that time. So in the passage before us. The prophet alludes to the approaching invasion of Nebuchadnezzar, and the utter impossibility of escape. They had been resting in false security, and made no preparation for such an invasion, when, in an unlooked-for moment, the king of Babylon approached with his army. While even some had cried peace, peace, there was no danger of war, even then the enemy was upon them, there was escape. They were powerless — no provision had been made for defense during the summer which then was past—the harvest had then gone, the summer ended, winter was at hand, the roads impassable — and there was no escape, they were not saved. They could neither prevent the invasion, nor escape from the enemy. They might as well be taken captive as to perish in the mountains in attempting to escape. This is evidently the meaning of the passage before us. Dr. Adam Clarke the Methodist commentator, has the following upon this passage:

" *The harvest is past.* The siege of Jerusalem lasted two years; for Nebuchadnezzar came against it in the ninth year of Zedekiah, and the city was taken in the eleventh. See 2 Kings xxv, 1–3. This seems to have been a proverb: We expected deliverance the first year — none came. We hoped for it the second year — we are disappointed; we are not saved — no deliverance is come."

# GOD ANGRY.

"God is angry with the wicked every day."—PSALMS vii. 11.

A misapprehension of the original meaning of these words, in connection with a false religious education, has led many to give to them an interpretation directly the reverse from what was intended by the writer. Our English version of the Scriptures represents God as being angry with the wicked every day, when the writer originally intended to teach the very reverse of this—that God was *not* angry.

No allusion was originally made to the wicked, in contradistinction from the righteous. The expression, "with the wicked," is printed in italics, indicating that these words were supplied by the translators, and not found in the original text. Allusion was made to the righteous, and though God judges the righteous daily, yet He is not angry with them.

Dr. Adam Clarke, the learned Methodist divine and commentator, has taken great pains to give us the different translations of this passage, some of which we here present, to show the different renderings:

The *Vulgate*.—"God is a judge, righteous, strong and patient. Will He be angry every day?"

The *Septuagint*.—"God is a righteous judge, strong and long-suffering; not bringing forth his anger every day."

The *Arabic* is the same as the *Septuagint*.

The *Genevan* version, printed by Barker, the king's printer, 1615, translates thus: "God judgeth the righteous, and him that contemneth God every day." On which there is this marginal note: "He doth continually call the wicked to repentance by some signs of his judgments."

Dr. Clarke then presents us his own views in the following language:

"I have judged it of consequence to trace this verse through all the ancient versions, in order to be able to ascertain what is the *true reading* where the evidence on one side amounts to a positive affirmation, 'God is angry every day,' and on the other side, to as positive a negation, 'He is *not* angry every day. The mass of evidence supports the latter reading. The Chaldee first corrupted the text by making the addition, *with the wicked*, which our translators have followed, though they have put the words into *italics*, as not being in the Hebrew text.

Several of the versions have read it in this way, 'God judgeth the righteous, and is *not* angry every day.'"

In the original text no reference is made to the *wicked*, and it is a gross perversion of the passage to interpret it so as to make it teach that anger exists in the bosom of our heavenly Father, towards any portion of his children. The meaning of the passage is, that God judgeth the righteous justly and continually, though He is not angry with them. Righteousness and judgment are the habitation of his throne; still his punishments are disciplinary, and his administration benevolent. His government is equitable, but He is not angry day by day with his children. According to the *Septuagint* version, God is a righteous judge, not bringing forth his anger every day. If He were an angry, passionate being, then He would not judge in righteousness. The meaning is, that, day by day, He is a righteous judge, and, therefore, *not* an angry God. The text originally taught an entirely different sentiment from what the translators make it teach. It taught that God was *not* angry every day, as were heathen deities, but was a just, good and righteous God.

# FURNACE OF FIRE.

"And shall cast them into a furnace of fire; there shall be wailing and gnashing of teeth."—MATT. xiii. 42.

THIS passage does not assert that the "furnace of fire" is in the future state of existence; and the context makes no reference to the condition of man after the resurrection. A brief allusion to the Scriptures will show that this expression was employed by the sacred writers to indicate temporal reverses and severe national judgments and calamities. The deliverance of the children of Israel from the oppressions of Pharaoh, was spoken of as an escape from an *iron furnace.* "But the Lord hath taken you, and brought you forth out of the iron furnace, even out of Egypt." Deut. iv. 20. "For they be thy people and thine inheritance, which thou broughtest forth out of Egypt, from the midst of the furnace of iron." 1 Kings viii. 51; Jer. xi. 4. The bondage in which Pharaoh held the Israelites, was figuratively represented to an *iron furnace.*

The judgments which came upon Jerusalem were spoken of under the figure of *furnace of fire.* That magnificent city was to be laid in ruins; the sword without and famine and pestilence within; and hence the expression: "The Lord's fire is in Zion, and his *furnace* in Jerusalem." Isa. xxxi. 9.

The following passage shows clearly that the national calamities which came upon Jerusalem were figuratively represented by a *furnace of fire.*

"And the word of the Lord came unto me, saying, Son of man, the house of Israel is to me become dross: all they are brass, and tin, and iron, and lead, in the midst of the furnace; they are even the dross of silver. Therefore, thus saith the Lord God, because ye are all become dross, behold, therefore, I will gather you *into the midst of Jerusalem,* as they gather silver, and brass, and iron, and lead and tin, into the midst of the furnace, to blow the fire upon it, to melt it, so will I gather you in mine anger, and in my fury, and I will leave you there and melt you. Yea, I will gather you, and blow upon you in the *fire* of my wrath, and ye shall be melted in the midst thereof. As silver is melted in the midst of the furnace, so shall ye be melted in the midst thereof; and ye shall know that I, the Lord, have poured out my fury upon you." Ezk. xxii. 17–22.

# DAMNATION TO HIMSELF.

"For he that eateth and drinketh unworthily, eateth and drinketh damnation to himself."—1 Cor. xi. 29.

Many have been religiously educated to believe that those who have made a profession of religion, and partaken unworthily of the communion, have been eating and drinking eternal damnation to their souls. But there was never a greater perversion of language than this. The apostle never designed to teach such a sentiment. The language he employed conveys no such meaning. Human creeds teach that the word "damnation" in the Scriptures means the endless ruin of the soul; and so strong are the religious prejudices of many, that it is extremely difficult to disabuse their minds of these erroneous interpretations.

The word rendered *damnation* in this passage, is *krima*, and is translated *judgment* and *condemnation*. It occurs in Matt. vii. 2, and is rendered *judgment:* "For with what judgment ye judge," etc. It occurs in Luke xxiii. 40, and is rendered there *condemna-*

*tion:* "Thou art in the same condemnation." In Luke xxiv. 20, it is applied to Christ, and is rendered *condemned:* "Deliver him to be condemned to death." Jesus, when on earth, made use of the same word, and applied it to himself, in John ix. 39: "For judgment *I* am come into this world." *Krima*, which is rendered *damnation* in the passage before us, is here translated *judgment.* The doctrine of endless punishment finds no support in this passage. The word "damnation" is too harsh a rendering of *krima;* it means temporal punishment, which was designed for the good of the offender. The succeeding verse shows what this *krima* was, or in what the punishment consisted, viz.: *weakness* and *sickness:* "For this cause many are weak and sickly among you, and many sleep." This was the punishment they brought upon themselves in eating and drinking unworthily. Those referred to, indulged in irregularities and excesses, so that they did not discern the Lord's body. Their sinful indulgences exposed them to temporal chastisement, and in this regard, they ate and drank unworthily.

The most intelligent orthodox commentators take this view of the subject, as the following quotations will show:

Whitby.—"*Damnation:* the word imports temporal judgments; and when St. Peter saith, the time is come, *arxasthai to krima*, that judgment must begin at the house of God, (1 Peter iv. 17), not damnation, surely. And this is certainly the import of the word here, (1), because the Corinthians did thus eat unworthily, and yet the judgments inflicted on them for so doing were only temporal, viz.; weakness, sickness and death, verse 30. (2), Because the reason assigned for those judgments is, that they might not be condemned in the other world, or that they might not be obnoxious to damnation."

Locke.—"Damnation, by which our translators render *krima*, is vulgarly taken for eternal damnation in the other world; whereas *krima* here signifies punishment of another nature, as appears by verse 30–33."

Pierce.—"*Krima* (damnation), signifies here, temporal punishment, viz.: weakness, sickness and death, as is plain from verse 30."

Clarke.—"*Krima*—judgment, punishment; and yet this is not unto *damnation;* for the judgment, or punishment, inflicted upon the disorderly and the profane, was intended for their emendation; for in verse 32, it is said, when we are judged *krinomenoi*, we are chastened, *paideuometha*, corrected as a father does his children, that we should not be condemned with the world."

# BURN AS AN OVEN.

"For behold, the day cometh, that shall burn as an oven; and all the proud, yea, and all that do wickedly, shall be stubble: and the day that cometh shall burn them up, saith the Lord of hosts, that it shall leave them neither root nor branch."—MAL. iv. 1.

"FIRE" was one of the most common figures in ancient times, to represent severe national judgments and calamities, and the overthrow and destruction of nations and cities. The destruction of the Jewish nation was spoken of under the figure of *burning* and of *fire*. And as the judgments came from the hand of God, as a merited retribution for sin, He was called a *consuming fire.*

"The Lord's *fire* is in Zion, and his *furnace* in Jerusalem." Isa. xxxi. 9. And again: "Through the wrath of the Lord of hosts is the land darkened, and the people shall be as the fuel of the *fire.*" Isa. ix. 19.

Divine judgments coming upon Jerusalem are spoken of as follows: "But if ye will not hearken unto me to hallow the Sabbath day, and not to bear a burden, even entering in at the gates of Jerusalem on the Sabbath day; then will I *kindle a fire* in the gates thereof, and it shall *devour the palaces of Jerusalem*, and it shall not be quenched." Jer. xvii. 27. See also Ezek. xxii. 18–22. We might refer to many other places where temporal destruction is spoken of under the figure of *fire*, and *flame*, and *burning*.

In the passage under consideration, national judgments are referred to, and when they came upon Jerusalem, that was the day that *burned as an oven*. The passage referred to the destruction of Jerusalem by the Romans, as admitted by Dr. Clarke, the Methodist commentator, and has no reference to the future world. He says:

"*The day cometh that shall burn as an oven*—the destruction of Jerusalem by the Romans. *And all the proud*—this is in reference to verse 15, of the preceding chapter. *The day that cometh shall burn them up*—either by famine, by sword, or by captivity, all these rebels shall be destroyed. *It shall leave them neither root or branch*—a proverbial expression for total destruction, neither man nor child shall escape."—*Com. on Mal.* iv. 1.

# HIDDEN TO THE LOST.

"But if our Gospel be hid, it is hid to them that are lost."—2 Cor. iv. 3.

A brief allusion to the context will exhibit the apostle's meaning. In the preceding chapter, he had been speaking of the two dispensations, contrasting the old and new covenants, and exhibiting the superiority of the Gospel over the Law. There was indeed some glory in the Law, but so great was the glory of the Gospel, that the Law appeared to have no glory by reason of the glory that excelleth! Moses was obliged to veil his face, because of the splendor of his countenance, which the Israelites could not look upon steadfastly. So there was a veil upon the hearts of the people; or, in other words, their minds were blinded, darkness rested upon their souls, which could only be removed by the light of the glorious gospel; hence, it was said, that this veil was done away with in Christ.

Now that the gospel was preached, nothing was concealed. Nothing was now hidden; all types and shadows were done away, and the gospel was proclaimed in all its fullness. And if its divine truths were not now perceived, it was because the people were willfully blind. If the gospel be hid, or *veiled*, so that people did not discover its divine excellency, they were lost; not endlessly lost, but *lost in sin;* their hearts were *veiled* by the errors to which they clung; their minds blinded by darkness and unbelief; and they were in a state of sin and degradation. Their state of sin was their lost state. Dr. Adam Clarke, the Methodist commentator, says, that "the word does not necessarily imply those that will *perish eternally*, but it is a common epithet to point out a man without the gospel and without God in the world."

"If our gospel be hid," or if its divine excellencies are not perceived—its heavenly truths seen and appreciated, it is because people wilfully close up the avenues to their souls, and shut out its light from their hearts, and obstinately remain blinded and lost. They were in darkness and unbelief. The gospel was plainly preached; and if it were obscure to any, it was because they closed their hearts against the light of truth, and preferring darkness to light, remained in a lost condition. And this was the moral state of the Jews. They were lost in sin—chose darkness rather than light, because their deeds were evil. Their minds were blinded and they would not come unto Christ, that they might have life. The passage under consideration has no reference to the future world, but the lost condition into which sin and error bring man in this life.

We present the following comments from Hammond, who believed in future punishment:

HAMMOND.—"For, by our preaching the gospel, we perform a very acceptable service to God, and bring in glory to his name, offer up a sweet-smelling sacrifice unto him, among all sorts of people, both among the penitent believers, which receive the faith, and live according to it, and the impenitent unbelievers, that receive it not. For though this sweet perfume, to the obstinate impenitent, hath been the most perfect poison, (as high perfumes sometimes are,) they have grown the worse for the gospel's coming among them; yet, to all that have forsaken their old courses of sin, and obeyed this call to a new life, it hath been the most comfortable vital savor that ever came to them. This is a weighty employment, and, unless God did particularly enable us, we never could be fit for it."

# DRAW BACK TO PERDITION.

"But we are not of them who draw back unto perdition; but of them that believe to the saving of the soul."—Heb. x. 39.

Many have erroneously supposed that this language refers to the immortal world, and the drawing back to perdition, means the misery of the soul in hell! It is supposed that the saving of the soul refers to the deliverance of man from endless punishment. This view of the subject is supported by human creeds, but not by divine revelation. The passage has no reference to the immortal world.

Those who abandoned the truth became unfaithful, and turned back again to the beggarly elements of Judaism, and suffered in the judgments which came upon the disobedient and sinful, were said to *draw back to perdition*, or to *destruction*, as the original is sometimes rendered. But Paul would have his brethren found faithful, and persevere unto the end, even to the saving of their lives.

We here present the opinions of several orthodox commentators upon this passage, as quoted by Paige:

LIGHTFOOT.—"As Christ's pouring down his vengeance, in the destruction of that city and people, is called his 'coming in his glory,' and his 'coming in judgment;' and as the destruction of that city and nation characterized, in Scripture, as the destruction of the whole world—so there are several passages that speak of the nearness of that destruction, that are suited according to such characters. Such is that in 1 Cor. x. 11, 'Upon us the ends of the world are come:' 1 Pet. iv. 7, 'The end of all things is at hand;' Heb. x. 37, 'Yet a little while, and he that shall come, will come, and will not tarry.'" —*Sermon on James* v. 9.

WAKEFIELD.—"But we are not they who withdraw unto destruction, but who faithfully persevere, to the deliverance of our lives."

CLARKE. "We are not cowards who slink away, and, notwithstanding, meet *destruction;* but we are *faithful,* and have our souls saved alive. The words *peripoiesis psuche* signify the *preservation of life,* see the note Eph. i. 14. He intimates, that, notwithstanding the persecution was hot, yet they should escape with their *lives.*"

# SON OF PERDITION.

"While I was with them (the disciples) in the world, I kept them in my name; those that thou gavest me, I have kept, and none of them is *lost*, but the son of perdition, that the Scripture might be fulfilled."—JOHN xvii. 12.

In whatever sense, Judas, the individual referred to here, was *lost*, that condition was essential to the fulfillment of the Scriptures! But, who will say that he must be consigned to endless perdition that the Scripture might be fulfilled? We are not aware that any Scripture required the endless punishment of Judas in order that it be fulfilled! Such an interpretation is too manifestly erroneous to require a moment's time to refute it.

The meaning of the passage is clearly this: while Christ was with the disciples, he kept them faithful to his cause, devoted to the work which engaged his attention;—and what is meant by his having lost none but the son of perdition, is, that none had abandoned his religion, except Judas, who betrayed him. Long before, one had been spoken of, who should lift up his heel against him. See

Psalms xli. 9. And when Judas turned away from his Lord and Master, that scripture was fulfilled, which declared that "he that eateth bread with me hath lifted up his heel against me."

When this disciple abandoned his Lord and Master, he was *lost* — lost to truth — lost in sin,— and because he was thus lost, he was called the son of perdition. It referred, simply, to his apostacy from the Christian faith, without regard to the future condition of Judas. Son of apostacy, means an apostate. Prof. Stuart says:

"The word *son* was a favorite among the Hebrews; and was employed by them to designate a great variety of relations. The son of anything, according to Oriental idiom, may be either, what is closely connected with it, dependent on it, like it, the consequence of it, worthy of it, etc. The son of eight days; that is, the child of eight days old; of a hundred years; that is, the person who is a hundred years of age; the son of my sorrow; that is, the one who has caused me distress; son of valor; that is, bold, brave; son of Belial; that is, a worthless man; son of wickedness; that is, wicked; son of a murderer; that is, a murderous person; son of death; that is, one who deserves death; son of thunder; that is, a man of powerful energetic eloquence or strength; son of peace; that is, a peaceable man."

Son of perdition, means an individual in an apostate condition — lost in sin.

We quote from "Paige's Selections," the following from eminent commentators upon this subject:

WHITBY.—"*And none of them is lost:* i. e., either by temporal death, chap. xviii. 9; or by falling off from me, but the son of perdition, i. e., Judas, worthy of perdition. So a *son of death* is one worthy of it, (2 Sam. xii. 5), and *ethnos apoleias* is a nation fit to be destroyed. Eccl. xvi. 9, Matt. xxiii. 15, and the note on Eph. ii. 2."

Dr. Whitby does not say what he understands by *perdition;* but the word *apoleias*, in the passage he quotes above, is precisely the word rendered *perdition* in the text. From the manner in which he uses that passage, he seems to have understood the word to imply temporal destruction, and nothing more.

ROSENMULLER.—"No one is ignorant that Judas is here intended, the betrayer of Christ, and who had fallen off from him. *Apoleia*, (perdition,) therefore, as the preceding words teach, in this place, seems to indicate a defection from Jesus, the teacher; as in 2 Thess. ii. 2, where the phrase *o uios apoleias* (the son of perdition) differs very little from *o uios amartias*, (the son of transgression), and is used concerning a noted imposter, who persuaded many to a defection from the Christian religion."

WAKEFIELD.—"*The son of mischief:* a Hebrew phrase for a *destructive*—*pernicious*—person; upon which mode of speaking, see my commentary on Matt. v. 9."—*Note in loc.*

HAMMOND.—"All this while of my continuing among them, I have labored, by revealing thy will to them, to confirm them, and also to preserve them from danger, and it hath succeeded well; of all those who were, by thy preventing grace, so prepared, as that they came to me, and undertook my service, none have carried or fallen off, (see chap. xviii. 9, and here ver. 15), but only the wicked traitor, prophesied of. Psalm cix."

# LOSE HIS OWN SOUL.

"For what is a man profited, if he gain the whole world, and lose his own soul? Or what shall a man give in exchange for his soul?"—MATT. xvi. 26.

THE word here rendered "soul," should have been rendered "life," as admitted by many of the most learned biblical divines, among whom we may mention Dr. Adam Clarke, the distinguished Methodist commentator. In fact, the original word occurs in the preceding verse, and is there rendered "life." "For whosoever will lose his *life*, for my sake, shall find it."

Jesus had just spoken of the dangers which those would encounter, who should make a public profession of his religion by taking up their cross and following him. They would receive such ill-treatment and persecution, that it would be like taking their lives in their hands and going forth to meet the enemy. The Savior knew well that this persecution would prevent some from embracing his religion, while others would turn away from him and abandon his cause, in order to escape persecution and *save their lives.* But such would even lose their lives; hence the expression, "whosoever will *save* his life, or attempt to save it, by joining hands with the persecutors, will lose it. And whosoever will lose his life for my sake, shall find it."

As though Jesus had said: "He who will accept my teachings, and obey my commands and instruction, and fearlessly meet danger and persecution, shall *save* his life; he shall be saved from destruction, when severe national judgments shall fall upon the persecuting Jew."

In the light of these suggestions, we readily apprehend the meaning of the passage under consideration. "For what is a man profited, if he shall gain the whole world and lose his own soul?" As though the Savior had said: "Suppose you reject my truth and gain the wealth and honors of the world, where is the *profit*, as you will certainly be overwhelmed in the terrible calamities about to come upon this sinful generation! Even admit that you will lose your life at the hand of the persecutor, for embracing my doctrine and religion, you can but lose it, and if you reject me, you certainly will lose it, hence there is nothing *gained* by rejecting *me.*"

This view of the subject is sustained by the parallel passage, recorded in the ix. chap. of Luke: "For what is a man advantaged if he gain the whole world and lose himself, or be cast away?"

Similar phraseology is found in the 10th chapter of Matthew, upon which Dr. Adam Clarke remarks as follows: "He that findeth his life shall *lose* it, was literally fulfilled in Archbishop Cranmer. He confessed Christ against the devil, and his eldest son, the Pope. He was ordered to be burnt, to save his life, he recanted, and was, notwithstanding, burnt." He denied the truth, to save his life, and then he lost it!

Learned orthodox divines of different names take this view of the subject.

CAMPBELL.—"*With the forfeit of his life:* English translation, *Lose his own soul. Forfeit* comes nearer the import of the original word, which Doddridge has endeavored to convey by a circumlocution, *should be punished with the loss of his life.* But the chief error in the English translation lies in changing, without necessity, the word answering to *psuche*, calling it, in the preceding verse, *life*, and in this, *soul.* The expressions are proverbial, importing, it signifies nothing how much a man gain, if it be at the expense of his life."

CLARKE.—"*Lose his own soul;* or *lose his life.* On what authority many have translated the word *psuche*, in the 25th verse, *life*, and in this verse, *soul*, I know not; but am certain it means *life*, in both places. If a man should gain the whole world, its riches, honors, and pleasures, and lose his *life*, what would all these profit him, seeing they can only be enjoyed during *life?*"

The legitimate sentiment here taught is, that we should not be so entirely absorbed in the pursuits of the world as to injure our physical constitutions and hasten ourselves into the grave. What does such a man *gain?* He has been consecrated to the world, amassed a large property; but *lost his life*. This we regard as the primary meaning of the passage under consideration.

# AGREE WITH THINE ADVERSARY

"Agree with thine adversary quickly, while thou art in the way with him; lest at any time the adversary deliver thee to the judge, and the judge deliver thee to the officer, and thou be cast into prison. Verily, I say unto thee, Thou shalt by no means come out thence till thou hast paid the uttermost farthing.—MATT. v. 25, 26.

THE meaning of this passage has been so entirely misapprehended, that some have erroneously supposed that Almighty God, who has created us for his pleasure, is our adversary. He is represented as our enemy, and that unless we do something quickly to appease his wrath and secure his favor, He will cut us off and throw us into the prison of hell, where we must remain eternally.

The language, however, clearly implies deliverance from prison, under certain circumstances, which shows conclusively that the punishment cannot be endless in duration. "Thou shalt by no means come out thence, till thou hast paid the uttermost farthing;" teaching clearly a release when the uttermost farthing was paid.

This proves nothing, therefore, in regard to endless punishment. Besides, God is not the adversary of man, but the Father of the world's great family, and a God of infinite love. He was prompted by the benevolence of his own nature to awaken man into existence, and has crowned that existence with tender mercies and loving kindness. "For his pleasure all things are and were created." He has opened his bountiful hand and scattered blessings along the pathway of humanity. In all our wanderings HE has never forgotten us, but has pitied us in our frailties and loved us while dead in trespasses and sins. He is good unto all, and his tender mercies are over all his works. And He is that God who will have compassion according to the multitude of his tender mercies. In a word, He is our FATHER, possessing all the moral qualities and perfections that belong to a good Father.

God, our heavenly Father, is not the adversary of man. He has created us in his own moral image, and loves us with a tenderness that surpasses the affection of a mother for her child.

The adversary alluded to in the passage under consideration, was a legal adversary, or an opponent at law. Reference was made to human tribunals and jurisprudence, and the penalty which follows negligence in the settlement of difficulties. It is better to come at once to some agreement with an adversary, and settle all disputes and difficulties immediately, rather than by delay and procrastination provoke the adversary to deliver thee to the officers of the law and be cast into prison. We are here admonished to avoid all such litigations. The subject has no reference to the future world, but to things pertaining entirely to this life.

Dr. Adam Clarke comments as follows on this passage:

"Those who make the *adversary* God, the *judge* Christ, the *officer* death, and the *prison* hell, abuse the passage, and highly dishonor God. Our Lord enforces the exhortation given in the preceding verses, from the consideration of what was deemed prudent in ordinary lawsuits. In such cases, men should make up matters with the utmost speed, as running through the whole course of a lawsuit must not only be vexatious, but be attended with great expense; and in the end, though the loser may be ruined, yet the gainer has nothing."

# WRATH OF GOD.

"For which things' sake the wrath of God cometh on the children of disobedience."—COL. iii. 6.

IN the Scriptures frequent reference is made to the "wrath of God." "Thou sendest forth thy wrath which consumed them as stubble." Ex. xv. 7. "My wrath shall wax hot." Ex. xxii. 24. "The day of the Lord cometh with wrath." Rev. vi. 17. Such language has been misunderstood and so falsely interpreted as to give to God the character of a merciless tyrant. Our heavenly Father has been represented as imbibing a hatred towards his own erring offspring, more terrible than ever dwelt in the bosom of the most depraved mortal that ever walked the earth. Hence, much of the worship and religious service in which people have engaged, has been designed to affect God, to placate his wrath, secure his favor and reconcile Him to man. Such views of God and religion have done great harm to Christianity and turned many away in disgust, from the Father of mercies, the God of our salvation. God cannot be angry, malignant, revengeful, and full of wrath, in any sense in which man is angry and wrathful, for "anger resteth in the bosom of fools." Eccles. vii. 9. And we are commanded to "cease from anger and forsake wrath." Ps. xxxvii. 8. Therefore God cannot indulge in any such sinful emotion himself.

When we read of the "wrath of God," we understand the language to be used in a figurative sense, to denote God's disapprobation of sin, his aversion to transgression, and his retributive justice. In the Scriptures, God is spoken of as a man, having the organization and passions of mortal beings; but all such language should be understood figuratively. We read of the "arm" and "hand" and "fingers" of the Almighty; of the "right arm" of the Lord, and of his "heart" and "breath;" that he "sits" and "rides" and "walks;" but these are all figurative expressions, adapted to the condition and circumstances of the ancient Hebrews, indicating the poverty of language in which ideas adapted to the comprehension of the people were conveyed, and were never designed to be understood literally.

To express the divine approbation of any course of action, expressions, similar to those employed by the people for a like purpose, must have been introduced, and therefore to represent God's disapproval of sin and its merited retribution, He is spoken of as being "angry" with the sinner, and exercised by wrathful emotions. Merited retribution indicated to their undeveloped and uncultivated minds, "anger" and "wrath" in God. When nations and individuals brought upon themselves swift destruction, pestilence, famine and war, such punishment was spoken of as a display of God's anger and wrath. It was so with Babylon, and Sodom and Gomorrah, and with Tyre and Sidon. They rebelled against God, forsook his ways and trampled upon his laws, and brought upon themselves swift destruction. Such chastisement is spoken of as a display of divine wrath. Hence, says Paul, "The wrath of God is revealed from heaven against all ungodliness and unrighteousness of men."

Macknight has some judicious remarks upon this subject, which we lay before our readers. He says:

"Thus, many words of the primitive language of mankind must have a twofold signification. According to the one signification, they denote ideas of sense, and according to the other they denote ideas of intellect. So that although these words were the same in respect of their sound, they were really different words in respect of their signification; and to mark that difference, after the nature of language came to be accurately investigated, the words which denoted the ideas of sense, when used to express the ideas of intellect, were called by critics *metaphors*, from a Greek word which signifies *to transfer;* because these words so used, were carried away from their original meaning to a different one, which, however, had some resemblance to it.

Having in the Scriptures these and many other examples of bold metaphors, the natural effect of the poverty of the ancient language of the Hebrews, why should we be either surprised or offended with the bold figurative language in which the Hebrews expressed their conceptions of the divine nature and government? Theirs was not a philosophical language, but the primitive speech of an uncultivated race of men, who by words and phrases taken from objects of sense, endeavored to express *their* notions of matters which cannot be distinctly conceived by the human mind, and far less expressed in human language. Wherefore they injure the Hebrews who affirm, that they believed the Deity to have a body, consisting of members of like form and use with the members of the human body, because in their sacred writings, the eyes, the ears, the hands, and the feet of God, are spoken of; and because he is represented as acting with these members after the manner of man.

'The voice of the Lord God walking in the garden.' Gen. iii. 8. 'The Lord is a man of war;' 'Thy right hand, O Lord, hath dashed;' etc.; 'The blast of thy nostrils.' Exod. xv. 3 –6–8. 'Smoke out of his nostrils;' 'Fire out of his mouth;' 'Darkness under his feet;' 'He rode;' and 'Did fly.' Ps. xviii. 8, 9, 10.

In like manner they injure the Hebrews who affirm they thought God was moved by anger, jealousy, hatred, revenge, grief, and other human passions, because in their Scriptures it is said: 'It repented the Lord;' 'It grieved Him.' Gen. vi. 6. 'A jealous God.' Ex. xx. 5. 'The wrath of the Lord.' Num. xi. 33. 'I hate.' Prov. viii. 13. 'The indignation of the Lord;' 'His fury.' Isa. xxxiv. 2. 'God is jealous;' 'Revengeth and is furious;' 'Will take vengeance;' and 'He reserveth wrath.' Nahum i. 2.

They also injure the Hebrews who affirm that they believe the Deity subject to human infirmity, because it is said: 'God rested.' Gen. ii. 2. 'The Lord smelled.' viii. 21. 'I will go down and see,' and 'if not, I will know.' xviii. 20. 'He that sitteth in the heavens shall laugh;' 'Shall have them in derision.' Ps. ii. 4. 'The Lord awaked,' etc. lxxviii. 65.

These and the like expressions are highly *metaphorical*, and imply nothing more but that in the divine mind and conduct, [to human perception,] there is somewhat analagous to, and resembling the sensible objects and the human affections, on which these metaphorical expressions are founded. If from the passages of Scripture in which the members of the human body are ascribed to the Deity, it is inferred that the ancient Hebrews believed the Deity hath a body of the same form with the human body, we must conclude they believed the Deity to be a tree, with spreading branches and leaves which afforded an agreeable shade; and a great fowl, with feathers and wings; and even a rock, because He is so called. Deut. xxxii. 15; Psa. xvii. 8, xviii. 2–31, and xci. 4."—*Macknight on the Epistles, Essay viii. Sec.* 1.

We should remember that the sentiments of the ancient Hebrews come to us clothed in oriental costume, and bold metaphorical expressions are employed to communicate their ideas. We read of the floods clapping their hands, and the hills skipping like lambs. This, of course, was highly figurative language. And so when we read of the wrath of God, we understand the language to be used in a figurative sense, to set forth the righteous retribution of God in the earth. Every transgression and disobedience received a just recompense of reward. The antediluvian world was swept away by a flood. Jerusalem was sacked by the Romans. Pharaoh and his hosts were swallowed up in the sea, and the cities of the plain were destroyed by divine judgment; and thus was the wrath of God revealed against the ungodliness and unrighteousness of men.

# CAST THE BAD AWAY.

"Again, the kingdom of heaven is like unto a net, that was cast into the sea, and gathered of every kind: which when it was full, they drew to shore, and sat down, and gathered the good into vessels, but cast the bad away. So shall it be at the end of the world, the angels shall come forth and sever the wicked from among the just; and shall cast them into the furnace of fire; there shall be wailing and gnashing of teeth."—Matt. xiii. 47–50.

This parable is found in connection with a series of parables in which Jesus represents the nature of his heavenly kingdom, the preciousness of his system of religion, the different classes of individuals who listened to his divine instructions, and the legitimate consequences which would follow a reception and rejection of his truth. Although the different illustrations which the Savior employed, are so varied as to be adapted to the comprehension of the people addressed, yet they all have a general application and similar meaning. The people were dull of apprehension, and, therefore, a variety of similitudes is introduced.

The kingdom of heaven, which is here spoken of, and which is frequently alluded to in the context, has reference to the economy of grace, or dispensation of truth, or system of religion, which Christ came to establish in the earth. By this kingdom being compared to a net, cast into the sea which gathered of every kind, we understand Jesus to reprensent the different classes of individuals who would make a profession of his heavenly truths, would accept his religion, and thus be gathered into his heavenly kingdom. These different classes are referred to in the parable of the *Sower*. Some joyfully accepted the truth, but through various influences, they fell away from it, and abandoned it. Riches choked the word with some, and others could not endure persecution; while others still remained true and faithful under every trial, even unto the end, and were saved from the terrible calamities which came upon those who abandoned the truth.

A separation is represented as taking place at the end of the world, or the *end* of the *aion age*, and *not* at the end of the *kosmos*—the material universe. Many mistake the meaning of the Savior, by erroneously supposing that he referred to the end of the material world, or universe.

In the original language, there are two words which are translated *world*, which we find in the immediate connection, viz.: *kosmos* and *aion.*

"The field is the world," verse 38, (*kosmos*). But when it says: "The harvest is the end of the world," verse 39; and "So shall it be in the end of this world," verse 40–49, we find that Jesus used a different word, viz.: *aion*, which clearly shows that he did *not* refer to the *end* of the material universe, for had he done so, he would have employed the word *kosmos*. *Aion* means age or time; an indefinite period of time. Donnegan, a Lexicographer, defines *aion* thus: "Time; a space of time; life-time and life," etc. The end of the *aion*, or the end of that *age*, referred to the time when severe national judgments would come upon the Jewish people for their sins, and all those who abandon the truth, or the kingdom, on account of persecution or through whatever other influences, would experience the just desert of their sins by suffering in the judgments which came upon that ungodly nation. Then a separation took place between the wicked and the just—so that not a single disciple perished—not a righteous man was overwhelmed in the destruction which came upon the Jews, as Eusebius, the historian, informs us. Dr. Adam Clarke, the Methodist commentator, says the same thing, thus:

"It is very remarkable that not a single Christian perished in the destruction of Jerusalem, though there were many there when Cestius Gallus invested the city; and had he persevered in the siege, he would have rendered himself master of it; but when he, unexpectedly and unaccountably, raised the siege, the Christians took that opportunity to escape."

Tne angels who went forth, were the messengers of his power, (for angel signfies messenger) commissioned to accomplish his work. By the wicked being cast into the furnace of fire, we understand to be meant a figurative representation of the awful judgments which come upon the inhabitants of Jerusalem, greater than ever had been or ever should be again. "The Lord's fire is in Zion, and his furnace in Jerusalem." See also Ezek. xxi. 17–22.

www.ingramcontent.com/pod-product-compliance
Lightning Source LLC
LaVergne TN
LVHW010220110826
845151LV00004B/1150

* 9 7 8 1 4 2 5 5 2 7 2 0 4 *